A Will is Not Enough in New York

SIMPLE, PRACTICAL THINGS
A NEW YORK RESIDENT CAN DO TO

- ❖ AVOID PROBATE
- ❖ AVOID GUARDIANSHIP
- ❖ PRESERVE ASSETS
- ❖ PROVIDE FOR HEALTH CARE
- ❖ PROVIDE FOR THE FAMILY'S CARE

By AMELIA E. POHL, ESQ.
and
New York Attorney
VINCENT J. RUSSO, ESQ.

EAGLE PUBLISHING COMPANY OF BOCA

The purpose of this book is to provide the reader with an informative overview of the subject; but laws change frequently and are subject to different interpretations as courts rule on the meaning or effect of a law. This book is sold with the understanding that the publisher and the authors are not engaging in, or rendering, legal, accounting, medical, psychiatric, financial planning or any other professional service. If you need legal, accounting, medical, psychiatric, financial planning or other expert advice, then you should seek the services of a licensed professional.

This book is intended for use by the consumer for his or her own benefit. If you use this book to counsel someone about the law or tax matters, then that may be considered to be an unauthorized and illegal practice.

WEB SITES: Web sites appear throughout the book. These Web sites are offered for the convenience of the reader only. Publication of these Web site addresses is not an endorsement by the authors, editors or publishers of this book.

EAGLE PUBLISHING COMPANY OF BOCA
4199 N. Dixie Highway, #2
Boca Raton, FL   33431
E-mail: info@eaglepublishing.com

Printed in the United States of America
ISBN 1-892407-52-3
Library of Congress Catalog Card Number: 2001098420

Introduction

Over the years, as we practiced law, we noticed that the questions people have about Wills, Trusts, Powers of Attorney, avoiding probate and guardianship, preserving assets, providing health care for themselves and their families, are much the same client to client. Many people are concerned about who will control their finances should they become too aged or ill to do so themselves. And of even more concern is their health care:

Who will make my medical decisions if I can't do so myself?
How can I pay for my health care?
How much and what type of insurance should I have?
How can I avoid guardianship?

Others worry about the care of family members. Those with minor children worry:

Who will care for my minor child if I become incapacitated or die?
Is there a way to make sure my child has enough money to see him through college?

Those with elderly parents worry:

How can I manage my parent's finances should my parent be unable to care for himself?
If my parent dies, will I need to go through Probate?
Is there a way to avoid Probate?

We agreed that a book answering such questions would be of service to the general public. We wish to thank all of the clients, whom we have had the honor and pleasure to serve, for providing us with the impetus to write this book.

SPECIAL THANKS
Many people contributed to the development to this book. We wish to give special thanks to Paul Adinolfi and Fred Adinolfi for their encouragement and assistance.

Vincent J. Russo, Esq.

VINCENT J. RUSSO is nationally recognized for his contribution and achievements in the field of Elder Law. Vincent is the manging shareholder of the law firm of Vincent J. Russo & Associates, P.C. of Westbury and Islandia, NY.

Vincent earned his law degree from Fordham University School of Law and a Masters of Law in Taxation from the Boston University of Law. He is admitted to the New York, Massachusetts and Florida State Bar Associations, and is a certified Elder Law attorney by the National Elder Law Foundation.

VINCENT J. RUSSO is a founding member, Fellow and past president of the National Academy of Elder Law Attorneys. He is a founding member and past chair of the Elder Law Section of the New York State Bar Association and is a member of the American Bar Association. He is past chair and founder of the Legal Advisory Committee to the Alzheimer's Assoc. Long Island Chapter, a member of the committees on Elder Law of the Nassau County and Suffolk County Bar Associations, chair of the Guardianship Committee as well as a former Board member of the United Cerebral Palsy Association of Nassau County.

Mr. Russo is the co-founder of the Theresa Alessandra Russo Foundation established in the memory of his daughter, Teresa. The Foundation supports creativity and Art For All Children by granting funds to Art/Music/Dance and Recreational programs for children with disabilities.

As a noted authority, author and lecturer in Elder Law, Mr. Russo has championed the rights of the elderly since 1985. He is a nationally recognized author, lecturer and authority in Elder Law. Vincent J. Russo is a frequent speaker at the Joint Conference on Law and Aging in Washington, DC. He has been keynote speaker at the Annual Conferences of the American Institute of Certified Public Accountants, the National Association of Professional Geriatric Care Managers, and the New Jersey Bar Association.

Vincent J. Russo has been the special guest on many radio and television programs, including CNN, NBC'S TODAY SHOW, CNBC, THE FOX NEWS NETWORK, CSPAN II and NEWS 12 LONG ISLAND.

Vincent J. Russo is the co-author of *New York Elder Law Practice* as well as Consulting Attorney for *When Someone Dies In New York*.

Mr. Russo has published numerous articles concerning the elderly and their families which have appeared in the New York State Bar Journal, the NAELA Quarterly, the New York State Queens County Bar Journal, the Long Island Examiner, ELDERCARE, a newsletter published by Eldercare, Ltd., the Elderlaw Report, Shepherd's Elder Care/ Law Newsletter, Personal Advantage/Financial published by Boardroom Reports,Inc.

A person with strong family values, Vincent makes his home in Lido Beach, NY with his wife Susan and their children.

For an illustration of some of Vincent's published materials, as well as his guest appearance on the "NBC Today Show" and other facets of his leadership in Elder Law, visit his Web site at: www.russoelderlaw.com.

Amelia E. Pohl, Esq.

Before becoming an attorney in 1985, AMELIA E. POHL taught mathematics on both the high school and college level. During her tenure as Associate Professor of Mathematics at Prince George's Community College in New York, she wrote several books including Probability: A Set Theory Approach, Principals of Counting and Common Stock Sense.

During her practice of law Attorney Pohl observed that many people want to reduce the high cost of legal fees by performing or assisting with their own legal transactions.

Attorney Pohl found that, with a bit of guidance, people are able to perform many legal transactions for themselves. Attorney Pohl utilizes her background as teacher, author and attorney to provide that "bit of guidance" to the general public in the form of self-help legal books that she has written.

Because there is such variation in the laws from state to state, each book written by Attorney Pohl is state specific.

Attorney Pohl is currently "translating" this book for the remaining states with the assistance of an attorney from each state who is licensed to practice in the given state.

Call EAGLE PUBLISHING COMPANY OF BOCA at (800) 824-0823 to learn of the availability of this book for any other state.

Reading the Law

Where applicable, we identified the state statute or federal statute that is the basis of the discussion. We did this as a reference, and also to encourage the general public to read the law as it is written. Prior to the Internet the only way you could look up the law was to physically take yourself to the local courthouse law library or the law section of a public library. Today all of the state and federal statutes are literally at your finger tips. They are just a mouse click away on the Internet. To look up a statute all you need is the address of the Web site and the identifying number of the statute.

 NEW YORK STATUTE WEB SITE
http://assembly.state.ny.us/ALIS

FEDERAL STATUTE WEB SITE
http://www4.law.cornell.edu/uscode

New York has consolidated their laws into 111 titles that are listed alphabetically. Each title is divided into numbered sections. For example:
(Surrogates 1750) refers to Section 1750 of the Surrogate's Court Procedure Act. (Estates 3-1.1) refers to Section 3-1.1 of the Estates, Powers & Trusts Law. (Dom. Rel. 73) refers to Section 73 of the Domestic Relations Law.

To look up a statute, all you need do is go to the Web site, find the title and then the section within the title. If you come across a topic that is of importance to you, then you may find it both interesting and profitable to read the law as it is actually written.

A Will is Not Enough in New York

CONTENTS

When You Need A Lawyer

The purpose of the book is to give the reader a basic understanding of New York law as it relates to Wills and other methods of Estate Planning. It is not intended as a substitute for legal counsel or any other kind of professional advice. If you have any legal question, then you should to seek the counsel of an attorney. When looking for an attorney, consider three things: EXPERTISE, COST and PERSONALITY.

EXPERTISE

The state of New York does not have a program to certify that an attorney is specialized in a particular area of law. However, attorneys are allowed to state that they are certified by an accredited institution, if such is the case. For example, the National Elder Law Foundation has a certification program for the field of Elder Law. An attorney certified by the Foundation, or other program such as being a Chartered Estate Planning Practitioner is allowed to make that fact known to the public.

There is a Lawyer Referral Service located in each county Bar Association. They can refer you to an attorney in your area who practices the type of law that you seek. You can get the number of the Lawyer Referral Service in your county by calling the State Bar of New York at (800) 342-3661.

One of the most reliable ways to find an attorney is through personal referral. Ask your friends, family or business acquaintances if they used an attorney for the field of law that you seek and whether they were pleased with the results. It is important to employ an attorney who is experienced in the area of law you seek. Your friend may have a wonderful Estate Planning attorney, but if you suffered an injury to your body, then you need an attorney experienced in Personal Injury.

Before employing an attorney, ask how long he has practiced in that branch of law and what percentage of his practice is devoted to that type of law.

COST

In addition to the attorney's experience, it is important to check what it will cost in attorney's fees. When you call for an appointment ask what the attorney will charge for the initial consultation and the approximate cost for the service you seek. Ask whether there will be additional costs such as filing fees, accounting fees, expert witness fees, etc.

If the least expensive attorney is out of your price range, then you can call your local county Bar Association for the telephone number of the Legal Aid office nearest you.

The New York State Bar Association has a directory of New York Legal Services Programs at their Web site.

 NEW YORK STATE BAR ASSOCIATION
http://www.nysba.org

PERSONALITY

Of equal importance to the attorney's experience and legal fees, is your relationship with the attorney. How easy was it to reach the attorney? Did you go through layers of receptionists and legal assistants before being allowed to speak to the attorney? Did the attorney promptly return your call? If you had difficulty reaching the attorney, then you can expect similar problems should you employ that attorney.

Did the attorney treat you with respect? Did the attorney treat you paternally with a "father knows best" attitude or did the attorney treat you as an intelligent person with the ability to understand the options available to you and the ability to make your own decision based on the information provided to you.

Are you able to understand and easily communicate with the attorney? Is he/she speaking to you in plain English or is his/her explanation of the matter so full of legalese to be meaningless to you?

Do you find the attorney's personality to be pleasant or grating? Sometimes people rub each other the wrong way. It is like rubbing a cat the wrong way. Stroking a cat from head to tail is pleasing to the cat, but petting it in the opposite direction, no matter how well intended, causes friction. If the lawyer makes you feel annoyed or uncomfortable, then find another attorney.

It is worth the effort to take the time to interview as many attorneys as it takes to find one with the right expertise, fee schedule and personality for you.

The Organization of the Book

Many people who have a Will think they have their affairs in order, reasoning that should they die everything will go the people named in the Will and somehow things will all be taken care of. But that is a simplistic view. There are many more things to consider.

1. What exactly will your beneficiaries inherit?
2. How will your property be transferred?
3. Can you (should you) avoid Probate?
4. Can you avoid a challenge to your Will?

The first four chapters of this book deal with these issues. Once you read theses chapters you will have a basic understanding of what will happen to your property should you die, regardless of whether you do, or do not, have a Will.

The rest of the book deals with things a Will cannot do:

Chapter 5. Manage your personal debt
Chapter 6. Limit your business debt
Chapter 7. Provide care for a minor or disabled child
Chapter 8. Appoint someone to make your health care decisions should you be unable to do so
Chapter 9. Appoint someone to handle your finances should you be unable to do so
Chapter 10. Help you qualify for MEDICAID should the need arise.
Chapter 11. Help your family settle your Estate.

A Will can't do these things but you will be able to do so once you read these chapters and understand what options are available to you under New York law.

GLOSSARY

This book is designed for the average reader. Legal terminology has been kept to a minimum. There is a glossary at the end of the book in case you come across a legal term that is not familiar to you.

FICTITIOUS NAMES AND EVENTS

The examples in this book are based loosely on actual events; however, all names are fictitious; and the events, as portrayed, are fictitious.

MALE GENDER USED

Rather than use he/she or himself/herself, for simplicity, we have used the male gender.

Your Estate Plan Check Up 1

To understand why ***A Will is Not Enough in New York*** you need to know what a Will can and cannot do. One thing a Will can do is make a gift of all you own (your ***Estate***). One of the things a Will cannot do is preserve and protect your property during your lifetime. For that, you need to think about risks to your property (poor investments, theft, loss through acts of nature, etc.) and what you can do to minimize or eliminate such risk. In other words, you need an ***Estate Plan*** for the care and management of your property during your lifetime.

The average person may protest "I don't have an Estate; none the less an Estate Plan." But you do. Everyone who has property, has an Estate Plan. You may never have verbalized your Estate Plan, or even thought about it, but it's there none-the-less. For example, take the case of the college student purchasing his first car. If his parents bankroll the purchase, the son may offer to hold the car jointly with them. The son's Estate is his car. His Estate Plan is to hold the car jointly with his parents so that they will own the car should anything happen to him.

This may not be the best Estate Plan. Holding the car jointly with his parents may make them liable for injuries or damages should the car be involved in an accident. If the young man's parents are familiar with New York law, they would be wise to refuse the offer and reassure their son "You can make a Will and make us the beneficiary of your car. But even if you die without a Will, we are your heirs under New York law. Either way we will inherit the car. Just make sure to drive carefully and carry enough car insurance."

This is a better Estate Plan. It gives the young man maximum control over his Estate (i.e., his car) during his lifetime. He can sell the car, mortgage it, or trash it, all as he sees fit. If he follows his parent's advice, of driving carefully and purchasing sufficient insurance, his Estate will have maximum protection. If he dies without a Will, and is single, without children, then under New York's *Rules Governing Intestate Succession*, his parents will inherit his Estate. And that is just the way the son wants things at this stage of his life.

Simple situation, simple Estate Plan. But, for most of us, life isn't all that simple. We may own many items of value and have loved ones who rely on us. At some point in our lives, we need to ask:

How can I make sure that my property will be inherited by my choice of beneficiary?

How can I arrange to have my property inherited quickly and at minimum cost?

How can I achieve these goals and yet have maximum control and protection of my property during my lifetime?

We will explore the different ways to answer these questions so that you can decide on an Estate Plan that is best for you. But before doing so you need to know what property you own; i.e., how much your Estate is worth. If you are married and your spouse handles all of the finances, it may be that you have no idea of the value of your Estate.

That was the case with Kristin. She met Matt when they were both at the pinnacle of their careers, but they had no more insight into their precarious position than fireworks in a summer sky, just before self-destruct.

Kristin was a model. Not the best, nor the most beautiful, but she made a comfortable living. She moved in a circle of famous models. She reflected off of their radiance, making her appear more attractive than she actually was.

Matt worked in middle management for one of those high tech companies. Like Kristin, he was not particularly gifted but he happened to be in Silicon Valley just at the time the high stakes investors were showing extraordinary, if not misguided, confidence in the industry. The good times were rolling. It never crossed Matt's mind that this would one day end. He spent the money as fast as it came in.

Kristin was impressed with the lavish gifts Matt gave to her. She, and her family, thought she made quite a catch when she announced her engagement. After the wedding she continued to model, but it took a lot of traveling and Matt resented her time away. Eventually, Kristin agreed to stop working altogether. After all, why should she, the wife of a wealthy man, need to continue with the rigors of a model's life of diet and exercise?

Matt never told Kristin about his financial difficulties. All she knew is that he was drinking quite a bit. Her suspicion that he also was into drugs was verified when he died, suddenly, because of an overdose. Her shock and sadness turned to anger when she discovered that all he owned was mortgaged; and he was heavily in debt. He even borrowed money from her family without her knowledge!

Matt's creditors took it all. The house, the boat, the Porsche, everything. If only Kristin had investigated the true state of their finances, she could have arranged to set aside the money she earned prior to her marriage and not end up as she did, a destitute widow, past her prime.

DETERMINING YOUR NET WORTH

Even if you are single you may not know the value of your Estate because you have not taken the time to actually sit down and figure it out. To get maximum benefit from this book, you need to take a few minutes to determine your *Net Worth* i.e. the current value of your Estate.

ASSETS:

$ _____ Cash (certificates of deposit, bank accounts, etc.)

$_____ Tangible personal property (jewelry, motor vehicles, private art, stamp or coin collections, etc.)

$_____ Cash value of insurance policies

$_____ Securities (stocks, bonds, mutuals, etc.)

$_____ Cash value of Pension Plans, IRA's, etc.

$_____ Cash value of a partnership or other business interest

$_____ Real property (residence, time share, lot, condo, cooperatives, etc.)

$_____ TOTAL VALUE OF ASSETS

It may be that you have a loan on your car or home, or any of the above items. You need to subtract away monies you owe to get the bottom line value of what you own:

LIABILITIES

$_____ Private loans

$_____ Mortgage Balance

$_____ Credit card debt

$_____ Car loan or car lease balance

$_____ TOTAL LIABILITIES

A simple subtraction gives you the value of your Estate.
ASSETS — LIABILITIES = NET WORTH

If you are married and hold all property jointly with your spouse, divide by 2 to get the value of your own Net Worth.

Your Net Worth is the value of all that you own, and that is how much your beneficiaries can inherit. Who will inherit your property depends on how your property is *titled* (held or owned).

There are three basic ways to title property:
⇨   in *your name only* - or -
⇨   *jointly* with another person - or -
⇨   you could hold property *in trust for* another.

The way your property is titled determines who will inherit that property:

> Property held in your **name only** will be inherited by the beneficiaries named in your Will.
> If you have no Will, the property will go to your heirs according to New York's Rules of Intestate Succession.
>
> Property you hold **jointly** will go to the surviving joint owner(s) of that property.
>
> Property held in **Trust** will go to those you name as the beneficiary of the Trust.
>
> NOTE ⇨ If you are married, your spouse may have rights in your property, regardless of the way your property is titled.

We will examine each of these types of ownership in detail so that you can give yourself an Estate Planning check-up, i.e., you can check whether the way you are currently holding your property accomplishes your Estate Planning goals.

MINE, ALL MINE

There's much to be said about holding property in your name only and not jointly or in trust for another. There's maximum control. You can sell it, trade it, mortgage it, with no one to account to, or ask "may I?" How you protect your assets depends on how much security you require. Again, it's all up to you.

As discussed, there are three things to consider when setting up an Estate Plan:

CONTROL   How to control and protect your
               Estate during your lifetime.
BENEFICIARY   How to be sure your Estate goes
               to the beneficiary of your choice.
COST   How to transfer your Estate to that
               beneficiary at lowest cost.

Holding all of your property in your name only should give you maximum control and protection; but such an Estate Plan may present problems with the cost of transferring your property upon your death. More than likely it will take some sort of court procedure to transfer that property once you die. The name of the court procedure is *Probate*. In New York, Probate is conducted in the Surrogates' Court (Surrogates 201). For simplicity, we will refer to the court that handles Probate as the *Probate Court*. We will refer to property that is transferred to your beneficiary by means of a Probate procedure as your *Probate Estate*.

Probate can be expensive, so if you keep all your property in your name only there could be a significant cost to transfer your property to the beneficiary of your Estate.

Holding property in your name should not create a problem with having your choice of beneficiary inherit your Estate, provided you have a valid Will. But if you die *intestate* (without a Will) the Probate Court will use New York's Rules Governing Intestate Succession to determine who gets your property. Of course it could be that the beneficiaries of your Estate under the Rules Governing Intestate Succession are exactly who you would have wanted, had you taken the time to prepare a Will. To help you determine if this is the case, we will take a few pages to explain the Law. Those who have a Will might want to skip over the section, however, this information is good to know in the event someone in your family dies without a Will. Once you read the section you will know whether you have a right to inherit their property.

THE FAMILY'S RIGHT TO INHERIT

The state of New York recognizes the right of the family to inherit property left by the *decedent* (the person who died); so the Rules of Intestate Succession cover all possible relationships beginning with the surviving spouse. In order for the spouse to inherit property under the Laws of Intestate Succession, the state of New York needs to recognize the union as a valid marriage.

Who Is Your Spouse?

In this era of people challenging the concept of the family unit, those of a philosophical bent may ponder the meaning of marriage. Is it a union of two people in the eyes of God? Is it even a union? Maybe it is just a contract between two people. The state of New York does not concern itself with such things. If a person dies without a Will, then the state will distribute the property according to the laws of New York; and the laws of New York determine whether two people are married.

BEING MARRIED IN NEW YORK

Under New York law, a marriage is a civil contract entered into voluntarily by a man and woman. To be married in New York means that a man and a woman have obtained a license to marry, solemnized the marriage by a civil or religious ceremony, and then lived together as man and wife.

New York law specifically prohibits the marriage of people:

☒ who are currently married to another person;

☒ who are **ancestors** (parent, grandparents, etc.) or **descendants** (child, grandchild, etc.) of each other;

☒ who are aunt and nephew or uncle and niece;

☒ who are brother and sister. This includes siblings who are half blood; i.e. they have only 1 parent in common (Domestic Rel. 5, 6, 10, 15).

New York law does not bar marriages between cousins.

NO COMMON LAW MARRIAGE

A Common Law marriage is one that has not been solemnized by ceremony. It is more than just living together. The couple must agree to live together as man and wife, and then publicly hold themselves out as being married, i.e., they tell people that they are married.

Many states do not recognize a Common Law marriage as being valid, and have passed laws to that effect. New York has not recognized Common Law marriages entered into in this state since April 29, 1933 (*Matter of Benjamin*, 34 N.Y.2d 27).

New York Courts respect the laws of other states and will recognize a Common Law marriage as being valid in New York if it was valid in the state where the couple entered into the marriage (*Mott v. Duncan Petroleum*, 414 N.E.2d 657).

NO SAME SEX MARRIAGES

There has been much discussion about whether the state should recognize marriage between people of the same sex. Vermont is the first state to recognize same sex marriages which they refer to as a "civil union."

Several states have passed statutes, specifically denying marital status to couples of the same gender regardless of whether that marriage is valid in any other state or country. New York has no such law as of the date we went to print, however, Courts have ruled that the surviving partner of a homosexual union is not considered to be a surviving spouse for purposes of New York's laws relating to Estates, Powers and Trusts (*Matter of Cooper*, 187 A.D.2d 128 (2d Dept. 1993).

Now that you know whether the State of New York considers you to be married, the next question is whether the state recognizes anyone as your descendant.

Who Is Your Child?

Medical technology has made important contributions to solving the problem of infertility. There are all sorts of solutions, from hormone replacement therapy, to sperm banks that provide donations anonymously, to frozen sperm and/or ova to be thawed and used at a later date, to women who become a surrogate or gestational mother. Solving a set of medical problems has opened the door to a new set of legal problems. Used to be, the only question was "Who's the father?" Now it could well be "Who's the mother? To answer these questions, the State of New York has passed laws to legally establish the parentage of children whose conception was assisted by medical technology. We will examine the law as it relates to the right of the child to inherit property.

CHILD OF ARTIFICIAL INSEMINATION

Under New York law, a physician may not use artificial insemination to impregnate a married woman unless both she and her spouse give their written consent. The physician who performs the technique must certify that he performed the procedure. Once the child is born, the father is listed on the birth certificate as the child's natural father; and that child has all of the rights as any other natural child born of his parents (Domestic Rel. 73).

A child born to a married couple using any other form of assisted conception has the same rights as a child conceived the old fashioned way. It is presumed that the husband consented to the assisted conception procedure. If that is not the case, and he is not the father of the child, he can *petition* (ask) the court to terminate his parental rights and responsibilities. If the husband is successful, the child will not be able to inherit from the husband, nor from his family.

THE SURROGATE PARENTING CONTRACT

A Surrogate Parenting Contract is an agreement, usually between a married couple and a woman, in which the woman agrees to be the birth mother of a child of the married couple. The child may be conceived using the sperm of the husband of the married couple, or the ovum of the wife of the married couple. Some states, such as Virginia, allow a couple to contract with a woman to have their baby. The court supervises the contract and then issues a birth certificate to the intended parents after the birth. This is not the case in New York. Surrogate parent contracts are prohibited as being against public policy. Anyone who participates in such a contract can be fined up to $500. Anyone who arranges such an agreement for a fee can be fined up to $10,000, and must forfeit the fee (Domestic Rel. 121, 122, 123).

In New York, any child born to a birth mother is the natural child of that birth mother. The birth mother may, after the child's birth, agree to an adoption. The Court may decide to allow the adoption, and if so, the child will have all of the rights as any other adopted child.

THE ADOPTED CHILD

An adopted child has the same rights to inherit property from his adoptive parents as does a natural child. The adopted child has no right to inherit property from his natural parents, or their family members. An exception is when the custodial parent of a child marries and the child is adopted by the step-parent. In such case, the child still has the right to inherit from that natural parent. For example, should a child be adopted by his stepfather, the child has the right to inherit from his stepfather and all of the stepfather's relatives and also from his mother and all of his maternal relatives (Domestic Rel. 117, Estates 1-2.10).

FROZEN SPERM AND THE AFTERBORN CHILD

Under New York law a child conceived prior to death and born to the surviving spouse after the death, has the same right to inherit under New York's Rules of Intestate Succession as any other natural child of the decedent (Estates 4-1.1 (c)). But suppose the child was conceived after death? That question is becoming more of an issue as couples are freezing sperm, ovum or preembryo (fertilized cell) for use at a later date. Often the purpose of the procedure is to protect the cell from damage during cancer treatments. If the treatment is unsuccessful, the surviving parent may decide to go ahead with the pregnancy using the frozen reproductive cell. This raises issues of whether the surviving parent has the right to so without the written consent of the deceased donor; and whether a child born of such procedure is entitled to inherit from the deceased donor.

This inheritance issue has important consequences, not only on the state level but on the federal level as well. A minor child who has lost a parent is entitled to Social Security benefits, but that those benefits are based on the state's Laws of Intestate Succession. Section 216 of the Social Security Act provides "a child's insurance benefits can be paid to a child who could inherit under the State's intestate laws." Specifically, a child cannot receive Social Security benefits, unless the child is entitled to inherit under the state's Rules of Intestate Succession.

This issue was brought before the Superior Court in New Jersey. The Court ruled that a child conceived and born after the death of a parent can inherit under New Jersey's Laws of Intestate Succession (*In Re Estate of Kolacy*, 322 N.J.Super. 593 (2000). Other states, such have passed laws on the issue. For example, under Virginia law, the child may not inherit from the deceased donor, unless prior to death the decedent agreed, in writing, to the implantation.

As of this writing there is no law in New York relating to the intestate rights of a child conceived after the decedent's death; however anyone can make provision in his Will for an afterborn child to inherit (or not to inherit) the Will maker's property.

If you decided to freeze your reproductive cells, it is important that you express, in writing, whether you want your cells used after your death. For those who are married, it is important that your spouse to join in the writing; i.e., that you have a written agreement as to the use and ownership of the reproductive cells in the event of divorce or the death of either party.

If you give permission for your reproductive cells to be used after your death, it is also important that you make a Will that includes a provision for a child conceived and born after your death to inherit your property; i.e., you need to state whether you do, or do not, want the child to inherit your property. If you do not make such provision, then under New York law, any child born after you make your Will is entitled to inherit as much as much as any of your other children (Estates 5-3.2).

See page 239 for an explanation of the right of an afterborn child to inherit property when a parent leaves a Will prepared before the child was born.

THE NON-MARITAL CHILD

A child born out of wedlock has the same rights to inherit from his/her natural father as does one born in wedlock, provided:

☑ the child's father married the natural mother, either before or after the birth. The marriage establishes the paternity even if it is later determined that the marriage was not valid; or

☑ a court issued a final order or judgment of paternity in this or any other state; or

☑ the father openly acknowledged the child as his own and it is generally known among his friends and family, that he is the father of the child;

☑ the father and mother signed an acknowledgment of paternity according to section 4135 (b) of New York's Public Health Law, and filed the acknowledgment with the Registrar; or

☑ the father acknowledged his paternity in writing in the presence of two witnesses and a notary public and then, within 60 days, filed the document with the New York State Department of Social Services. (Domestic Rel. 24, Estates 4-1.2).

The Rules of Intestate Succession are based on the right of family members to inherit property from the decedent. Now that we know who the state of New York considers to be your spouse and child, we can examine how much of your Estate each is entitled to inherit.

RULES GOVERNING INTESTATE SUCCESSION

Should you die with property titled in your name only, and without a Will, then the state of New York provides one for you in the form of the Rules Governing Intestate Succession. Once your debts, funeral and administrative expenses are paid, whatever is left (your **net Probate Estate**) is distributed as follows:

✧ MARRIED, NO CHILDREN ✧

If you are married with no surviving descendant (child, grandchild, great-grandchild, etc.), your net Probate Estate goes to your surviving spouse (Estates 4-1.1 (a)(2)).

✧ NOT MARRIED, WITH CHILDREN ✧

If you are single, and have descendants, they will inherit your Probate Estate **by representation** (Estates 1-2.16). "By representation" is one of those technical terms that is best explained through example.

ALL CHILDREN SURVIVE

Suppose a decedent is unmarried, and has 4 children, Ann, Barry, Carl, David. If he dies without a Will, his net Probate Estate is divided equally between his children; i.e. each get 25%.

CHILD WITHOUT DESCENDANTS DIES BEFORE DECEDENT

If Ann dies before her father leaving no descendants, then Barry, Carl and David divide the Probate Estate between them. Each get one third.

CHILDREN WITH DESCENDANTS DIES BEFORE DECEDENT

Suppose instead that only Carl and David survive their father. If Ann dies leaving 2 children and Barry dies leaving 3 children, then the Probate Estate is divided into 4 shares — one for each surviving child and one share for each deceased child who left descendants. Carl and David each get their share, namely, Carl gets 25% of the estate and David gets 25%. The remaining 50% is divided equally among the five grandchildren, each receiving 10% of the Probate Estate.

✧ MARRIED WITH CHILDREN ✧

If you have a surviving spouse and children, your spouse takes $50,000, plus half of your net Probate Estate. Your children inherit the other half, by representation (Estates 4-1.1 (a)(1)).

✧ SINGLE, NO CHILDREN ✧

If you have no surviving descendant, your net Probate Estate will be divided equally between your parents. Your parent's right to inherit can be challenged if your parent failed or refused to provide for you during your formative years (under the age of 21). If your parent later made amends and established a parent-child relationship that continued to your death, then the Court may decide that your parent has the right to inherit your property (Estates 4-1.1(4), 4-1.4).

If only one your parents is alive, then your Probate Estate goes to that parent. If neither parent is alive, your Estate goes to your brothers and sisters by representation. Siblings who share only one parent (a half brother or half sister) inherit the same as if they were siblings of whole blood (Estates 4-1.1 (4), (5) and (7b)).

If you have no surviving brothers, sisters, nephews or nieces, your net Probate Estate is divided in half with half going to your next of kin on your mother's side and the other half going to your next of kin on your father's side.

✧ NEW YORK: HEIR OF LAST RESORT ✧

Property that is either unclaimed or abandoned, goes to the state, so if you die without a Will and you have absolutely no next of kin, the state of New York will "inherit" your Probate Estate (Estates 4-1.5).

CAUTION   IT ISN'T ALL THAT SIMPLE

The explanation in this book of the laws of Intestate Succession is abridged. Even though you may now know more about New York's Rules Governing Intestate Succession than you ever wanted to know, there is much more to the law. For example, we did not explain exactly who gets your property if you are not survived by if you are not survived by a spouse, descendants, parents or their descendants. New York statute (Estates 4-1.1 (6) and (7)) explains the order of distribution in such case but that statute is complex. If you are concerned about the inheritance of your property at this level should you die without a Will, you can consult with an attorney who can explain the law to you. Better yet, have your attorney prepare a Will for you so that your property will go to the beneficiary of your choice, and not according to New York's Rules Governing Intestate Succession.

THE COST OF PROBATE

Holding property in your name only gives you maximum control and protection during your lifetime. If you do not like the way your property will be distributed should you die without a Will, then you can control who inherits your property by preparing a Will. But there is still the question of what it will cost to transfer your Estate to your beneficiaries. In all probability, a Probate procedure will be necessary. How much of your Estate will need to be spent to Probate your Estate?

THE SMALL ESTATE AFFIDAVIT

There is no need to be concerned about the cost of Probate if you have no real estate in your name only, and the value of all of your personal property (bank accounts, securities, etc.) is $20,000 or less. The beneficiary of your Estate can get possession of your property by taking the death certificate to the Clerk of the Surrogate's Court in the county of your residence. The Clerk will give your beneficiary an *Affidavit* to complete. An Affidavit is a written statement in which the *Affiant* (the person making the statement) tells someone with authority to administer an oath (the Clerk or a Notary Public) that the statements in the Affidavit are true and correct. Once the Clerk verifies that the beneficiary is entitled to the property the Clerk will issue a *Short Certificate* authorizing the Affiant to take possession of the property.

If you are married, and the sum of your personal property is not greater than $30,000, that property can be transferred to your spouse in the same manner, i.e., by Affidavit (Surrogates 1301, 1302, 1304, 1310).

OTHER ITEMS TO THE SURVIVING SPOUSE

Under New York law, your surviving spouse, or if no spouse, your minor child (i.e. child under 21) is entitled to keep the following household items:

⇨   All household furniture, appliances, computers, and musical instruments up to $10,000 in value;

⇨   the family bible, family pictures, video tapes, computer tapes and software, up to $1,000 in value;

⇨   any domestic animal with food for 60 days, 1 tractor, 1 lawn tractor, up to $15,000 in total value.

In addition, your surviving spouse, or if no spouse, your minor child, can take title to any motor vehicle, held in your name only, provided the value of your car is not greater than $15,000. All your spouse (or child) need do is take a certified copy of the death certificate to the nearest Department of Motor Vehicles, sign an Affidavit and pay any necessary transfer fees (Estates 5-3.1).

TO SUMMARIZE:
The following items can be transferred with a Short Certificate:

⇨   bank accounts and certificates of deposit;

⇨   state income tax refund;

⇨   securities (stocks, bonds, mutual funds, etc.)

⇨   final wages due to the decedent;

⇨   money or property held by a hospital, nursing home or residential care facility;

provided the total value is not greater than $20,000 ($30,000 if there is a surviving spouse). In addition, the surviving spouse is entitled to keep household items as above described and a car up to $15,000, and all without the need for a full Probate procedure (Surrogates 1310).

Things are not so simple if you own real property in your name only or if you own personal property in your name only in excess of $20,000 ($30,000 if married). There will need to be a Probate procedure which involves appointing someone, a **Personal Representative**, to take possession of your Probate Estate, pay valid bills and taxes, and then distribute whatever is left to the proper beneficiary.

The root of the word Probate is "to prove." It refers to the first step in the Probate procedure, that is, to examine proof of whether you left a valid Will. If you leave a valid Will naming someone to serve as Executor or Personal Representative, the Court will appoint that person for the job and issue **Letters** giving him authority to settle your Estate (Estates 1-2.13). If you die without a Will, the Court will appoint your surviving spouse to serve as Personal Representative. If your spouse is unable or unwilling to serve, or if you are single, then New York statute gives the following order of priority:

1. your child
2. your grandchild
3. father or mother
4. sister or brother
5. anyone entitled to the largest share of
   your Estate (Surrogates 1001).

If two or more people have equal priority and they cannot agree who should serve as Personal Representative, then the Court will make the decision.

The full Probate procedure is involved and time consuming; not to mention, expensive. Administration of the Estate can take anywhere from several months to more than a year, depending on the size and complexity of the Estate. Your Personal Representative must take possession of your Probate Estate and prepare an inventory of your Estate. Where necessary he will need to employ an appraiser to evaluate the property.

Your Personal Representative must notify all of your creditors that they have a right to come forward and file a *claim* (i.e. a demand for payment) for monies that you may owe. He may decide to publish notice in the newspapers to be sure all creditors are notified of their right to file a claim with the Court (Surrogates 1801).

It is the responsibility of the Personal Representative to see that the Probate procedure is conducted properly. If the Personal Representative makes a mistake, he may be responsible to pay for that mistake. For example, if he pays a debt that did not need to be paid — or if he transfers property to the beneficiaries too quickly and there were still taxes due on the estate, he may need to pay for that mistake from his own pocket (Estates 11-4.7).

To avoid mistakes, the Personal Representative needs to employ an attorney to guide him through the process. It then becomes the attorney's job to see to it that the Estate is administered according to New York law and without any liability to the Personal Representative. The attorney's fee is a proper charge to your Estate. And there may be other charges to your Estate, as well:

$$ Court fees to file the Probate procedure

$$ The cost of a bond that the Court may order
for the protection of your Probate Estate

$$ The cost of notifying your creditors which may
include publishing notice, or mailing notice
to them by registered or certified mail

$$ The cost of an appraisal

$$ Accounting fees to prepare an inventory,
and account for monies spent during the
Probate procedure

$$ The cost of transferring property to the proper
beneficiary, i.e., recording deeds, broker fees
to sell securities or real estate.

PERSONAL REPRESENTATIVE'S FEES

The Personal Representative is entitled to reasonable compensation for his work in settling the Estate. Under New York statute, what is considered reasonable is based on the amount received and then paid out:

> 5% commission on receiving and
>   paying out the first $100,000;
> 4% commission on the next $200,000;
> 3% commission on the next $700,000;
> 2 1/2 % on the next 4 million;
> 2% on anything over 5 million dollars.

ATTORNEY'S FEES

The Probate Court must approve the amount paid to the Personal Representative's attorney; but in general, attorney's fees are much the same of those of the Personal Representative (Surrogates 2110, 2307).

Once all valid claims, taxes and the costs of the Probate procedure (including attorney and Personal Representative fees) are paid, whatever is left is distributed to the proper beneficiary and the Personal Representative will close out the Estate.

You may be thinking that Probate is a good thing to avoid. Why should your Personal Representative go through all that effort to settle your Estate? Why should your beneficiaries wait months or maybe more than a year to inherit maybe 90% (or less) of your Estate?

There are different ways to arrange your Estate so that your beneficiaries can immediately inherit your Estate without incurring unnecessary costs. In the next two chapters we will examine each of these methods in detail.

robate Necessary? 2

Many people think that only wealthy people need to make plans to avoid Probate, yet each year, heirs of relatively modest estates, spend thousands of dollars to settle an Estate. A bit of Estate Planning could have eliminated most, if not all, of the cost (and hassle) suffered by those families.

If you have a small Estate and only one or two beneficiaries, then it is not all that difficult to arrange your finances to eliminate the need for Probate altogether. All you need do is title your property so that it automatically goes to your beneficiaries. There are many ways to arrange your finances to get this result. The most common method is to hold property jointly with another. Such an arrangement is the Estate Plan of choice for most married couples. Husband and wife often hold all of their property jointly, so that the surviving spouse has complete and immediate access to their property without any need for Probate.

Holding property jointly may not be the most desirable method for the single person, or the surviving spouse who is now single. There are other ways to ensure that your property is inherited quickly and without cost to your heirs. In this chapter we explore the pros and cons of different methods of holding property so that it can be transferred without the need for Probate.

PROPERTY HELD JOINTLY

Bank accounts, securities, motor vehicles, real property can all be owned by two or more people. If one of the owners of the property dies, then the surviving owner(s) continue to own their share of the property. Who owns the share belonging to the decedent depends on how the ownership was set up. If the title to the property indicates that the owners are *Joint Tenants with survivorship,* then should one of them die, the remaining owner(s) own the property.

If title to the property indicates that they are *Tenants-In-Common*, then there is no right of survivorship. Should one of the owners die, his share will go to whoever he names as beneficiary under his Will, or if no Will then according to the Rules of Intestate Succession.

THE JOINT BANK ACCOUNT

When two or more people open an account, the agreement will state whether they hold the account as Joint Tenants with right of survivorship, or as Tenants In Common.

In general, any account held jointly, is a survivorship account if each owner has the ability to withdraw funds on his own signature because should one owner die, the survivor can withdraw all of the funds in the account and close it out (Banking 675).

For example, suppose all you own is a bank account and you want whatever you have in this account to go to your son and daughter when you die. You might think that a simple solution is to put each child's name on the account, but first consider the problems associated with a joint account.

⊠   POTENTIAL LIABILITY
If you hold a bank account jointly with your adult child and that child is sued or gets a divorce, then the child may need to disclose his ownership of the joint account. In such a case, you may find yourself spending money to prove that the account was established for convenience only and that all of the money in that account really belongs to you.

⊠   OVERREACHING
Making your child a joint owner of the account gives the child free access to the account. Monies may be withdrawn without your knowledge or authorization. You may be thinking that couldn't happen because you would immediately know of the withdrawal, and you could force the child to return the money. That may be true when you are healthy and alert. But in this ever aging society, it is likely that you will live to an advanced age and not be as aware as you are today.

That was the case with Amanda. All she had when her husband died, was a bank account worth $50,000. She wanted to be sure that the money would go to her two sons, Robert and Leon, without the need for Probate. She went to the bank with her two sons and opened a new survivorship account with all three names on the account as joint owners.

Several years passed without incident. As Amanda aged, her health began to fail, and she became more and more dependent on Robert. She needed his assistance to take her to the doctor, to do her shopping, and of course take care of her finances. Robert had a wife and two children, so it was hard for him to care for his family and his mother as well. Leon was single, yet he never seemed to have the time to help care for his mother. And Robert resented that.

Finally, Amanda died. Just after the funeral, Leon asked Robert about the bank account:

"Didn't Mom have a joint account in our names?"

"Yeah, but I closed it out. There was only a few thousand left, and I used it for her funeral."

Leon thought it strange that all of the money was gone, so he went to the bank and asked to see the record of withdrawals. He found that over the last two years Robert had written several large checks to himself. There was only $7,000 left in the account when Robert closed it out, within a week of her death.

Leon fumed for several weeks before he brought up the subject. Robert's face flushed when Leon asked about the money. Leon did not know if it was from anger or embarrassment. He soon learned that it was both when Robert asked "Where were you for the past two years? You never once helped. Did you know she became incontinent at the end? Who cleaned up? Not you. She blessed me every day. She often said she would have been dead long ago if it wasn't for me. She wanted me to have that money!"

"Mom never said anything to me about wanting you to have the money. She never asked for my help and neither did you. It isn't right for you to throw this up to me now."

The boys never spoke of the money again. But then there were few times that they ever spoke to each other after that.

Because of these inherent problems, you might want to hold the funds in your bank account so that your beneficiary does not gain access to the monies unless you die while the account is active. You can do so by opening a **Benficiary Account**.

THE BENEFICIARY ACCOUNT

When opening an account with a bank you can give directions to the bank about what to do with the account should you die. If you do not give any such directions, and the account is in your name only, then should you die while the account is open, the monies in your account will become part of your Probate Estate and will be distributed in the same way as any other item that you hold in your name only.

One way to avoid Probate of the account yet retain full control of the account during your lifetime, is to open a beneficiary account. You can do by setting up an *In Trust For* ("ITF") account. Your contract with the bank will direct that, upon your death, the account funds are to be given to one or more beneficiaries that your name.

THE IN TRUST FOR ACCOUNT

If you open an In Trust For account, then unless your contract with the bank states differently:

⇨ During your lifetime you are free to withdraw from the account, or even close the account, without asking the beneficiary's permission to do so.

⇨ The beneficiary has no right to make withdrawals from the account during your lifetime.

⇨ If you hold the account in trust for two or more beneficiaries, the funds will be divided equally among the beneficiaries who survive you. (Estates 7-5.1, 7-5.2, 7-5.7).

You can set up an account that you hold jointly with your spouse so that it is held "In Trust For" one or more beneficiaries. For example:

Eldon Smith and Lorraine Smith,
as JOINT TENANTS WITH RIGHT OF SURVIVORSHIP
IN TRUST FOR Eldon Smith, Jr. and Fred Smith

Unless the contract with the bank states differently, under New York law:

⇨ The children (Eldon, Jr. and Fred) have no right to the account during the lifetime of their parents.

⇨ If either Eldon or Lorraine dies, then the surviving spouse owns the account, and is free to close the account or change the beneficiary of the account.

⇨ Once Eldon and Lorraine are deceased, their sons share the money in the account equally.

⇨ If one of the children dies before the surviving parent dies, then the remaining son gets all of the money in the account (Banking 675, Estates 7-5.6).

A Will is Not Enough in New York

Companies that sell securities usually offer a similar arrangement. You can arrange to have a security (a stock, bond or securities account) transferred to a beneficiary upon your death. You can instruct the holder of the security to **Pay On Death** ("POD") or *Transfer On Death* ("TOD") to a named beneficiary. As with the "In Trust For" account, the TOD registration has no effect on the ownership of the security until the owner of the security dies; for example:

TANYA BEDDIE TOD FRED BEDDIE

Fred has no right to the security during Tanya's lifetime. Once Tanya dies, all Fred need do is produce a certified copy of the death certificate to have the security transferred to him.

If your Estate consists only of bank accounts and/or securities, and you want all of your property to go to one or two beneficiaries without the need for Probate, but with maximum control and protection of your funds during your lifetime, then holding your property in any of these beneficiary forms:

> "In Trust For"
> "Pay-On-Death"
> "Transfer-On-Death"

should accomplish your goal.

REAL PROPERTY HELD JOINTLY

If you own real property together with another, then who will own the property upon your death depends on how the current owner is identified on the face of the deed. The first paragraph of the deed should identify the person who transferred the property to you (the **Grantor**). The person to whom the property was transferred is called the **Grantee**. The deed might read something like:

> This indenture, made this day, May 1, 2001, between ROBERT TRAYNOR, party of the first part, and
> SUSAN CODY and HENRY TRAYNOR
> as JOINT TENANTS, party of the second part,
> . . .

Robert Traynor (party of the first part) is the Grantor of the deed. He transferred the property to Susan Cody and Henry Traynor who are the Grantees and the present owners of the property. Because the deed identifies Susan and Henry as JOINT TENANTS they have rights of survivorship. Should one of them die, the other will own the property 100%. The survivor need do nothing to establish the ownership, but both names remain on the deed. The surviving owner can have a certified copy of the death certificate recorded in the county where the property is located. Once recorded, the public records will show that there is now just one owner.

🗎 DEED WITH A LIFE ESTATE

A *Life Estate* interest in real property means that the person who owns the Life Estate has the right to live in that property until he/she dies. You can identify a Life Estate interest by examining the face of the deed. If somewhere on the face of the deed you see the phrase RESERVING A LIFE ESTATE, then the Grantee cannot take possession of the property until the owner of the Life Estate dies. For example, suppose the granting paragraph of the deed reads:

This indenture, made this day June 2 ,2000
between JOSE CAVALLO,
party of the first part, and
SALVATORE CAVALLO
party of the second part,

. . .

RESERVING A LIFE ESTATE
TO JOSE CAVALLO

. . .

Jose Cavallo (the Grantor) is the owner of the Life Estate. Salvatore Cavallo (the Grantee) is the owner of the *Remainder Interest.* Salvatore has no right to occupy the property during Jose's lifetime. Once Jose dies, Salvatore will own the property and is free to take possession of the property, sell or transfer it, as he sees fit.

If you are an owner of the Life Estate interest, upon your death, no Probate procedure will be necessary to transfer the property to the owner of the Remainder Interest.

📋 DEED HELD AS TENANTS IN COMMON

You might have a deed that names you and another person as Grantee, followed by TENANTS IN COMMON. In such case, there is no Right of Survivorship. Should you die, your share of the property will go to whomever you named as beneficiary of that share in your Will. If you die without a Will, the Rules Governing Intestate Succession determine who will inherit your share.

If your deed does not say whether you are a Joint Tenant or Tenant In Common, then according to New York statute you hold title as Tenants in Common (Estates 6-2.2). Should you die, a Probate procedure will be necessary to determine who has the right to inherit your share of the property.

📋 DEED HELD AS HUSBAND AND WIFE

If you are married and own real property together with your spouse, then the deed should reflect the fact that you are married, such as in the following example:
TODD AMES AND SUSAN AMES, HIS WIFE
or
TODD AMES AND SUSAN AMES, HUSBAND AND WIFE
or
TODD AMES AND SUSAN AMES, TENANTS BY ENTIRETY

If you own property together with your spouse, should one of you die (and providing you are still married), the surviving spouse will own the property 100%. The name of the deceased spouse remains on the deed, so the surviving spouse needs to record a certified copy of the death certificate. Once recorded, anyone examining title to the property will know that there is now one owner (Estates 6-2.2 (b), (c)).

No Probate procedure will be necessary if you hold property in New York:

⇨　as a Joint Tenant with right of survivorship - or -

⇨　as the owner of a Life Estate - or -

⇨　as Tenant By The Entirety

In each of these cases, upon your death, the surviving owner will own the property 100%. If there is a Probate procedure for other property owned by the deceased Grantee, then a title search at the time of transfer will reveal the fact that the Grantee died. If no Probate is necessary, then all the surviving Grantee need to do is to keep a certified copy of the death certificate, and receipts showing that all applicable Estate Taxes have been paid, to present at closing should the surviving Grantee decide to sell or transfer the property.

Even though nothing need be done to establish the ownership of the surviving owner, it is a good idea to have a certified copy of the death certificate recorded in each county where the decedent owned real property. Once the death certificate recorded the decedent's name is, in effect, removed from the deed.

WHEN PROBATE IS NECESSARY

If you own New York property in your name only, or as a Tenant-In-Common, it will take a Probate procedure to transfer property to your intended beneficiary. As explained in Chapter 1, the type of Probate procedure will depend on the size of your Estate.

OUT OF STATE PROPERTY

This chapter relates only to property that you own in New York. If you own property in another state or country, then the laws of that state or country determine who has the right to inherit property in that state. Whether or not there are rights of survivorship depend on the laws of that state. Some states require that the deed specifically state that there are rights of survivorship. In such states, a deed held as Joint Tenants (and no stated right of survivorship) is the same as a Tenancy In Common.

If you own out of state property jointly with another, it is important that you check with an attorney in that state to be sure that your share of the property will go to the person of your choice.

If you are married, and own property in your name only, you need to be aware that your spouse may have rights in your property. That is the case in Community property states, but other states may have Dower rights or other statutory rights as a surviving spouse. In the next chapter, we will discuss the statutory rights of a surviving spouse in real property located in New York. But if you are married and own property in your name only in another state, you need to determine the rights of your spouse in that state.

Still another concern is whether a Probate procedure will be necessary to transfer out of state property that you own to your beneficiary.

TRANSFERRING OUT OF STATE PROPERTY

Each state is in charge of the way property located in that state is transferred. Most state laws are similar to New York namely, property you hold as a Joint Tenant with Right of Survivorship or property in which you hold a Life Estate interest are transferred without the need for Probate. Property you own as a Tenant In Common or in your name only may require a Probate procedure in order to transfer the property to your beneficiary.

If you own property in your name only in this state and in another state, upon your death it may be necessary to have a Probate procedure in New York, and an ***ancillary*** (secondary) Probate procedure in the state where the property is located. This could have the effect of doubling the cost of Probate.

Still another problem with out of state property is the matter of taxes. Some states have an inheritance or transfer tax. Estate taxes may be due in the state where the property is located as well as in New York. It may be necessary to file a tax return in two states. In addition to increased taxes, this can double the cost of the accounting fees.

If you own property in another state, it is important to consult with an attorney to learn the answers to all of these questions, namely:

Who will inherit my property under the laws of the state where it is located?

Will a Probate procedure be necessary to transfer that property to my beneficiaries?

Will a state tax need to be paid?

If you find that Probate will be necessary to transfer real property that you own in New York or elsewhere, you may decide that the cost of Probate is too expensive. You may be tempted to go for the quick fix of having the deed to the property changed so that you are joint owners with the intended beneficiary of the property; or you may decide to transfer the property to your beneficiary and keep a Life Estate for yourself.

This will avoid Probate, but it may not be the best Estate Plan because you will not have maximum control over the property during your lifetime. If you hold real property as a Joint Tenant With Right of Survivorship or as a Life Tenant, you will not be able to sell that property during your lifetime without getting permission from your beneficiary. And if the beneficiary gives permission and the property is sold, the beneficiary will have the legal right to share in the proceeds of the sale.

You may be thinking "I can make my son joint owner of my home and avoid any need for Probate. I trust him to do what I want with the property. If I decide to sell, I know he won't ask for any part of the proceeds regardless of his legal right to those funds."

And all that may be true, but it may cost you more in taxes to sell your property than if you kept the property in your name only.

Under today's law, you can sell your home without paying a Capital Gains tax, provided you lived there for 2 of the prior 5 years and the Capital Gains on the sale is not greater than $250,000 ($500,000 if married). If you sell your home after making the Life Estate transfer (or making your child a Joint Tenant), then unless your child occupies the home as his primary residence, his share of the property is subject to a Capital Gains tax.

If your son does not take his share of the proceeds, then why should he pay any Capital Gains tax?

In such case, you'll be the one to pay the tax on your son's share of the proceeds.

Is there a better way to avoid Probate?

Maybe. Read on.

How To Avoid Probate 3

TRUE OR FALSE?

(   )   If you have a Will, then Probate will be necessary.

(   )   Probate will be necessary if you don't have a Will.

(   )   Probate will be necessary if you are single and own more than $20,000.

If you answered false to all of the above, you are either a lawyer, or you carefully read the last chapter.

All of these sentences are false because you may have arranged your property so that it passes to your beneficiaries automatically, without the need for Probate. The point we were attempting to make is that:

> Whether a Probate procedure is necessary has nothing to do with whether there is a Will, or even how much money is involved. The determining factor is how the property is titled (owned).

There are three basic ways to title property:

- ✧ in your name only
- ✧ jointly with another
- ✧ in trust for another

Chapter 1 examined the pros and cons of holding property in your name only, with the biggest "con" being that Probate may be necessary. In Chapter 2 we noted that holding property jointly with another solved the Probate problem, but at the sacrifice of the control and protection offered by keeping property in your name only. In this Chapter we examine another option which may be the solution to these problems.

39

A full Probate procedure may be necessary if you hold personal property in your name only which is worth more than $20,000, or if you hold real property as a Tenant-In-Common or in your name only. We explored different ways to re-title property to avoid Probate, but these methods may have trade-offs that are unacceptable to you. One way to avoid many of these potential problems is to set up a **Revocable Living Trust** (also known as an **Inter Vivos Trust**).

A Revocable Living Trust is designed to care for your property during your lifetime and then to distribute your property once you die without the need for Probate. You may have been encouraged to set up such a Trust by your financial planner, attorney, or accountant. Even people of modest means are being encouraged to use a Trust as the basis of their Estate Plan. But Trusts also have their pros and cons. Before getting into that, let's first discuss what a Trust is and how it works:

SETTING UP A TRUST

To create a Trust, an attorney prepares the Trust document in accordance with the client's needs and desires. The person who signs the document is called the **Trustor** or **Settlor.** If the **Trustor** also funds the Trust, then he is also referred to as the **Grantor.** We will refer to the Revocable Living Trust as the "Living Trust" or just the "Trust" and the person setting up the Trust as the "Grantor." The Trust document identifies who is to be the Trustee (manager) of property placed in the Trust. Usually the Grantor appoints himself as Trustee so that he is in total control of property that he places into the Trust. The Trust document also names a Successor Trustee who will take over the management of the Trust property should the Trustee resign, become disabled or die.

Once the Trust document is properly signed, the Grantor transfers property into the Trust. The Grantor does this by changing the name on the account from his individual name to his name as Trustee. For example, if Elaine Richards sets up a Trust naming herself as Trustee, and she wishes to place her bank account into the Trust, then all she need do is instruct the bank to change the name on the account from ELAINE RICHARDS to:

ELAINE RICHARDS, TRUSTEE of the ELAINE RICHARDS REVOCABLE TRUST AGREEMENT DATED JULY 12, 2001.

When the change is made, all the money in the account becomes Trust property. Elaine (wearing her Trustee hat) has total control of the account, taking money out, and putting money in, as she sees fit. Similarly, if she wants to put real property into the Trust all she need do is have her attorney prepare a new deed identifying her as the Grantee/Trustee as above described.

The Trust document states how the Trust property is to be managed during Elaine's lifetime. Should Elaine become disabled, the Trust will provide for her Successor Trustee to take over and manage the Trust property. Because the Trust is revocable, if she wishes, Elaine can terminate the Trust at any time and have the Trust property placed back into her own individual name. If she does not revoke her Trust during her lifetime, then once she dies the Trust becomes irrevocable, and her Successor Trustee must follow the terms of the Trust Agreement as it is written. If the Trust says to give the Trust property to certain beneficiaries, then the Successor Trustee will do so. If the Trust directs the Successor Trustee to continue to hold property in Trust and use the property to take care of a member of Elaine's family, then the Successor Trustee must do so.

THE PROS

A Living Trust has many good features.

☆ AVOID PROBATE

As discussed in Chapter 1, Probate can be time consuming and expensive. Both the Personal Representative and his attorney are entitled to payment for their services. These fees can be significant. It may be necessary to hire accountants and appraisers, as well. If you have property in two states, then two Probate procedures may be necessary (one in each state) and that will increase the cost of Probate. If the Trust is properly drafted and your property placed into the Trust, you should be able to avoid Probate altogether.

☆ AVOID A CHALLENGE TO YOUR ESTATE PLAN

A Trust operates much like a Will because it provides for the distribution of your Estate when you die. Unlike a Will, it is not subject to Probate, so no Court is charged with the duty of "proving" that your Trust is valid. Your Successor Trustee can distribute your property as you direct, without asking anyone's permission to do so, and without giving the Court or any outside party an opportunity to examine the document. This does not mean that your Estate Plan cannot be challenged. It can. But if the Trust is drafted according to New York law, and not for the purpose of avoiding your creditors, or cutting off your spouse's right to inherit, it will be very difficult for anyone to challenge the document.

✪ CARE FOR FAMILY MEMBER:

You can make provision in your Trust to care for a minor child or family member after you die. If your family member is immature or a born spender, you can set up the Trust to protect the beneficiary from squandering the inheritance. If you are concerned that your beneficiary will spend, within months, what it took you a lifetime to earn, consider having an attorney prepare a Trust that will spread the inheritance over an extended period of time. Your Trust can direct the Trustee to give a certain amount of money every 5 or 10 years; for example you can direct the Trustee to give part of the gift when the beneficiary reaches 25, another amount when he reaches 35, and then 45, etc.

If your intended beneficiary has a creditor problem, you can set up a *Spendthrift Trust*. You can direct your Successor Trustee to use the Trust funds for your beneficiary's health care, education, and living expenses, and nothing else. With a properly drafted Spendthrift Trust provision the Trust funds should be protected from the claims of the creditors of the beneficiary.

NO CREDITOR PROTECTION FOR GRANTOR

You can set up a Spendthrift Trust for a beneficiary so that the beneficiary's creditors cannot force payment for monies owed by your beneficiary. But you cannot set up a Spendthrift Trust for yourself. Property held in your Revocable Living Trust is freely accessible to you, it is likewise accessible to your creditors both before and after your death. If you die owing money, your creditors can have a Personal Representative appointed to locate funds to pay those debts. The Personal Representative can require that your Trust property be used to pay for those debts (Estates 7-1.5, 7-3.1, Surrogate's 1002(1)).

☆ PRIVACY

Your Trust is a private document. No one but your Successor Trustee and your beneficiaries need ever read it. If you make a gift of real property in your Will, then your Personal Representative will have a certified copy of your Will recorded in the county in New York where the property is located (Surrogates 2506). Once recorded, your Will becomes a public document. Anyone can examine the county records, read your Will and see who you did (or did not) provide for in your Will.

Even if your Will makes no gift of real property, once the Will is filed with the Surrogates' Court it is open to public scrutiny — as are other Probate documents such as the inventory of your Probate Estate, creditor's claims, etc. It is not much of a stretch to predict that in the future, Court records will be available on the Internet!

LEASE SAFE DEPOSIT BOX AS TRUSTEE

Another privacy issue is what happens to the contents your safe deposit box, should you become disabled or die. Under New York law, only the person who is leasing the safe deposit box can access that box. The bank will not allow anyone else to look at the contents of the box without a Court order. Any member of your family can get a Court order to examine the contents of your box. The order will require that a bank employee be present when the contents of the safe deposit box are examined.

One of the benefits of having a Living Trust, is that you can lease the safe deposit box in your name as Trustee with instructions to the bank to allow your Successor Trustee free access to the safe deposit box in the event of your incapacity or death. By doing so you can avoid having the bank officer (or anyone other than your Successor Trustee) look at the contents of your safe deposit box.

✰✰ AVOID GUARDIANSHIP

Once you have a Trust you do not need to worry about who will take care of your property should you become disabled or too aged to handle your finances. The person you appoint as Successor Trustee will take over the care of the Trust property if you are unable to do so. If you do not have a Trust and you become incapacitated, a Court may need to appoint a Guardian to care for your property. The cost to establish and maintain the guardianship is charged to you. And, as we will see in Chapter 9, that can be even more expensive than a Probate procedure.

With all these perks, you may be ready to call your attorney to make an appointment to set up a Trust, but before doing so there are a few things you need to consider.

THE CONS

⊠ COMPLEXITY

A Trust is a fairly complex document, often 20 pages long. It needs to be that long because you are establishing a vehicle for taking care of your property during your lifetime, as well as after your death. Your Trust may be written in "legalese," so it may take you considerable time and effort to understand it. It is important to have your Trust document prepared by an attorney who has the patience to work with you until you fully understand each paragraph of the document and are satisfied that what it states is what you really want.

⊠ PROBATE MIGHT STILL BE NECESSARY

The Trust only works for those items that you place in the Trust. If you own property as a Tenant-In-Common it may be necessary to transfer your share of the property to your beneficiary. If you purchase a security in your name only, without a "Transfer On Death" designation to your Trust, or to some other beneficiary, then a Probate procedure may be necessary to determine who should inherit your security.

The attorney who prepares the Trust usually creates a safety net for such a situation. He prepares a Will for you to sign at the same time you sign the Trust. The Will makes your Trust the beneficiary of your Probate Estate. If you own anything in your name only, and a Probate procedure be necessary, the Will directs your Personal Representative to make that asset part of your Trust by transferring the asset to your Successor Trustee. Your Successor Trustee will add that asset to your Trust (Estates 3-3.7).

The Will prepared by the attorney is called a **Pour Over Will** because it is designed to "pour" any asset titled in your name only, into the Trust. Having the Will ensures that all of your property will go to the beneficiaries named in your Trust. But the downside of holding property in your name only is that a full Probate procedure may be necessary just to get that asset into your Trust. If avoiding Probate is your goal, holding property, in your name only, defeats that goal.

You can ensure that a Probate procedure will not be necessary by transferring your assets into your Trust during your lifetime, but if you neglect to put something into your Trust, the Pour Over Will stands by to make the transfer of that asset into your Trust.

⊠ YOU MAY NEED YOUR SPOUSE'S PERMISSION
   ## TO TRANSFER PROPERTY INTO YOUR TRUST

Many married couples prepare a Trust as part of their overall Estate Plan. Sometimes a married person has a Trust that was prepared prior to the marriage, or he may decide to create a Trust to care for children from a previous marriage. In such case, it may be necessary to have the spouse agree, in writing, to transfers into the Trust. The reason permission is needed is the **Elective Share**. The Grantor's spouse has a right inherit at least as much as allowed under New York law, unless the spouse signs a waiver, or a prenuptial or postnuptial Agreement.

In New York the Elective Share is equal to $50,000 or one-third of the **Net Estate** of the decedent spouse, whichever is greater. The Net Estate is the sum of:

⇨ Property held in the decedent's Trust, and

⇨ The Probate Estate less the cost of the Probate procedure; funeral expenses and all valid claims (but not including Estate taxes); and

⇨ Nonprobate transfers such as from joint bank accounts, "In Trust For" accounts, "Transfer On Death" securities, and

⇨ Gifts made by the decedent within one year of his death (Estates 5-1.1 A).

If you make transfers into your Trust without your spouse's permission, and without providing for the Elective Share, your surviving spouse can go to the Surrogates' Court and demand that as much property be transferred from the Trust (or from anyone in possession of your property) as is necessary to make up that Elective Share.

⊠ COST

Because of the thoroughness of the document and the fact that it is custom designed for you, a Trust will cost much more to draft than a simple Will. In addition to the initial cost of the Trust, it can be expensive to maintain the Trust should you become disabled or die. Under New York statute, a Trustee is entitled to an annual commission based on the value of the Trust property:

First $400,000: $10.50 per $1,000 or major fraction thereof.
Next $600,000: $4.50 per $1,000 or major fraction thereof.
Over 1 million: $3.00 per $1,000 or major fraction thereof.

In addition, the Trustee is entitled to a commission of 1% of the value of Trust principal that is paid out and commission on income earned by Trust property. See Surrogates 2309 and 2312 for the schedule of commissions paid on income.

A Trustee also has the right to charge for any specialized services he performs. If you choose an attorney to be your Successor Trustee, he has the right to charge the above commissions, and also to charge for any legal work he performs. A financial institution can charge to serve as Successor Trustee, and also to manage the Trust portfolio.

You may decide to appoint your spouse or a family member as Successor Trustee, who may want little, or no, compensation. But regardless of who you choose to be Successor Trustee, you need come to an agreement as to what will be charged to manage the Trust. If you choose a professional (lawyer, accountant, financial planner, etc.) your agreement needs to include fees for work that may be done in his/her professional capacity.

The fee agreement should be in writing and signed by you and your Successor Trustee. The fee agreement can be included in the Trust document with a provision that whoever accepts the job of Successor Trustee, agrees to accept the fee as provided in the Trust document. If you do not make written provision for fees, then under New York law, the Trustee is entitled to be compensated according to the statutory schedule (Surrogates 2309, 2312).

⊠ ☆ THE TRUST IS LEGALLY ENFORCEABLE

Any beneficiary of the Trust can petition the Surrogates' Court to settle a dispute arising out of the administration of the Trust. For example, if the Trustee is not properly administering the Trust, the beneficiaries can petition the Court to remove the Trustee and appoint another to serve as Successor Trustee (Estates 7-2.6).

We gave this section a cross and a star, because the right to have a Trust enforced or administered by a court is a double edged sword. It is great to have the Court protect the rights of your beneficiaries, but the cost of a Court battle could be greater than using Probate to transfer your Estate. Worse yet, your beneficiaries are at a disadvantage because the Trustee can charge the legal expenses to your Trust, while the beneficiaries must pay for their legal battles out of their own pocket. Even if the beneficiaries win the argument, the Trustee's legal fees are paid from the Trust, so there is just that much less for the beneficiaries to inherit.

TAXES AND YOUR TRUST

Putting property into a Revocable Living Trust does not shield that property from taxes. All of the property held in a Revocable Living Trust is taxed as if the Grantor were holding that property in his/her own name. If the property earns income, then income taxes will be due, and at the same rate as the Grantor would have paid if he had no Trust. Once the Grantor dies, both the federal and state government have the right to impose an *Estate Tax* on property transferred to a beneficiary as a result of the death. All the property owned as of the date of death becomes the decedent's *Taxable Estate*. This includes real property (homestead, vacant lots, etc.) and personal property (cars, life insurance policies, business interests, securities, IRA accounts, etc.). It includes property held in the decedent's name alone, as well as property that he held jointly or in Trust. It also includes gifts given by the decedent during his lifetime that exceeded $10,000 per person, per year. That *Annual Gift Tax Exclusion* is now based on the cost of living index and in 2002 was increased to $11,000.

For most of us, this is not a concern because no federal Estate Tax need be paid unless the decedent's Taxable Estate exceeds the federal *Estate Tax Exclusion* amount. That amount is currently one million dollars and is scheduled to go even higher:

YEAR	ESTATE TAX EXCLUSION AMOUNT
2002-2003	$1,000,000
2004-2005	$1,500,000
2006-2008	$2,000,000
2009	$3,500,000

In 2010 the federal Estate Tax is scheduled to be phased out altogether; however in 2011, the Estate Tax will be reinstated unless lawmakers change the tax law once again.

A TRUST TO REDUCE ESTATE TAXES

Under current law, Estates of those who die in 2010 are exempt from Federal Estate taxes, but in 2011, the Estate Tax is scheduled to be reinstated and Estates worth more than $1,000,000 will once again be subject to a sizeable Estate Tax. A couple with an Estate in excess of a million dollars can reduce the risk of an Estate Tax by setting up his and her Trusts, so that each person can take advantage of his own Estate Tax Exclusion.

For example, if a couple owns 2 million dollars, they can separate their funds into two Trusts each valued at one million dollars. The Trusts can be set up so that a surviving spouse can use the income from the deceased partner's Trust for living expenses. In this way, their standard of living need not be reduced by separating their funds into two Trusts.

If they do not wish to separate funds, they can set up a single Joint Trust that separates into two Trusts once one partner dies. Again, the surviving spouse is free to use the income from both Trusts. Once both partners are deceased, the beneficiaries of their respective Trusts will inherit the funds, hopefully with no Estate Tax due.

If the couple make no Trust provision, and they hold their property jointly, then the last to die will own the two million dollars with only one Estate Tax Exclusion available.

A Revocable Living Trust is a relatively simply way for a married couple to reduce, if not eliminate, the need to pay Estate taxes, however, there is still the problem of the federal Gift Tax and the Capital Gains Tax.

THE UN-UNIFIED GIFT TAX

Up until the year 2002, if you gave someone more than $10,000 in any given year you had to report that gift to the IRS. The Annual Gift Tax Exclusion is now adjusted for the cost of living and is $11,000 for the year 2002. The IRS keeps count of amounts that you give over the Annual Gift Tax Exclusion. Although you are required to report the gift, no tax need be paid unless that running total is more than the federal Estate Tax Exclusion amount. If your running total does not exceed that amount during your lifetime, once you die, the cumulative value of gifts reported to the IRS will be added to your Taxable Estate.

Up until the change in the tax law in 2001, the Gift and Estate tax were unified. No Gift Tax needed to be paid unless the total value of the taxable gifts exceeded the federal Estate Tax Exclusion amount. That changes in 2004. In 2004, the Estate Tax Exclusion amount goes up to $1,500,000, but the amount for the Gift Tax Exclusion remains at $1,000,000, so they are no longer unified.

To summarize:
If you make a gift to anyone that is greater than the Annual Gift Tax Exclusion for that year, you must report the gift to the IRS. The IRS keeps a running count of gifts you made in excess of the Annual Gift Tax Exclusion. In 2004, if that sum exceeds $1,000,000, you will pay a Gift Tax on any amount that you give that is over the Annual Gift Tax Exclusion.

The Estate Tax is scheduled to be repealed in 2010, but not the Gift Tax.

The current federal Estate tax is scheduled to be phased out in the year 2010, but a new Capital Gains Tax is scheduled for 2010 that may prove even more costly than the Estate Tax. The new Capital Gains tax is related to the way inherited property is evaluated by the federal government. Real and personal property is inherited at a "step-up" in basis, meaning that if the decedent's property has increased in value from the time he acquired it, the beneficiary will inherit the property at its fair market value as of the decedent's date of death. For example, if the decedent bought stock for $20,000 and it is worth $50,000 as of his date of death, the beneficiary will take a step-up in basis of $30,000; i.e. the beneficiary inherits the stock at the current $50,000 value. If the beneficiary sells the stock for $50,000, he pays no Capital Gains tax. If the beneficiary holds onto the stock and later sells it for $60,000, the beneficiary will pay a Capital Gains tax only on the $10,000 increase in value since the decedent's death.

Up to 2009, there is no limit to the amount a beneficiary can take as a step-up in basis. But in 2010 caps are set in place. The decedent's Estate will be allowed a 1.3 million dollar step-up in basis, plus another 3 million for property passing to the surviving spouse (IRS Code 1022(b)). The new law could result in significant Capital Gains taxes that the beneficiary must pay. For example, suppose in 2010 you inherit a business from your father that he purchased for $100,000 and it is now worth 2 million dollars. There is a capital gain of 1.9 million dollars, but you are allowed a step-up in basis of only 1.3 million. If you sell it for 2 million dollars $600,000 of your inheritance will be subject to a Capital Gains tax.

We will discuss methods of reducing the Gift Tax and the Capital Gains Tax in Chapter 7.

Although many methods can be used to transfer property without the need for Probate, it may be each method has a downside that is objectionable to you. Maybe you don't have enough money to warrant the cost of setting up the Trust at this time. Holding property jointly with another may raise issues of security and independence.

Holding bank accounts or securities in beneficiary form (In-Trust-For or Pay-On-Death) may not be as flexible as you wish. This is especially the case if you want to give gifts to several charities or to minor children. For example, suppose all you own is a bank account that you hold In-Trust-For your son. If you ask your son to use some of that money for your grandchild's education it may be that your grandchild gets none of the money. Not necessarily because your son disregarded your wishes, but maybe he is sued or falls upon hard times. If you keep your property in your name only and leave a Will giving a certain amount of money for your grandchild, the child will know exactly how much money you left and the purpose of that gift.

After taking into account all the pros and cons of avoiding Probate, you may well opt for a Will and a Probate procedure. If you make such a decision, it is important to keep in mind that Estate Planning is not an "all or nothing" choice. You can arrange your Estate so that certain items pass automatically to your intended beneficiary, and other items can be left in your name only, to be distributed as part of a Probate procedure. By arranging your finances in this manner, you can reduce the value of your Probate Estate, and that in turn should reduce the cost of Probate.

In the next chapter, we discuss the Will as an Estate Planning tool.

Those of you who have a Will may be thinking that there is no reason to read the Chapter, but does your Will:

- Make provision for the amount to be paid to your Personal Representative?
- Make gifts of your personal property? (jewelry, car, etc.)
- Name a guardian to care for your minor child?
- Make adjustment for gifts or loans that you gave to the beneficiaries of your Will?
- Give specific instructions about how your bills are to be paid; i.e., which of your beneficiaries will have his inheritance reduced in order to pay your debts?

Has your Will been prepared so that it will be difficult for anyone to challenge it?

Have you stored your Will so that it is safe AND easily accessible to you during your lifetime and to your Personal Representative after your death?

If you answered "Yes" to all of the above questions, then you can skip over to Chapter 5.

Your Will – Your Way 4

Many people decide that the Will is the best route to go but do not act upon it, thinking it unnecessary to prepare a Will until they are very old and about to die. But according to reports published by the National Center for Health Statistics (a division of the U.S. Department of Health and Human Services) 2 of every 10 people who die in any given year are under the age of 60. Twenty percent may seem like a small number until it hits close to home as it did with a young couple.

Alex and Cathy were an old-fashioned couple in a modern world. When they married, they knew they wanted a large family. There was no question that Cathy would stay home and raise the children while Alex went to work. Luckily he did very well as one of the managers of a string of restaurants. Better yet, he enjoyed his work. He loved to cook and would even take over the kitchen when he returned from work. That suited Cathy just fine because she had her hands full raising their three boys.

Cathy couldn't help thinking how lucky they were that morning as she fixed breakfast. A nice house. Healthy, if not rambunctious boys. All in all a comfortable marriage. Her only concern that day was the fact that Alex was flying off on a business trip. All this terrorist news made her nervous about flying. Alex reassured her that it was only an hour's flight, and besides he was flying the company plane and not a commercial airliner.

But it was not terrorists that brought down the plane, just a malfunctioning rudder.

THINGS A WILL CAN DO

Though we all agree that one never knows, still people put off making a Will, figuring that if they die before getting around to it, New York law will take over and their property will be distributed in the manner that they would have wanted anyway. The problem with that logic is the complexity of New York's Rules Governing Intestate Succession. If you are survived by a spouse, child, parent or sibling, then it isn't too difficult to figure out who will inherit your property. But if none of these survive you, the ultimate beneficiary of your property may not be the person you would have chosen, had you taken the time to do so.

Others think that it is not necessary to have a Will because they have arranged their finances so that all of their property will be inherited without the need for Probate. But money could come into your Estate after your death. This could happen in any number of ways from winning the lottery and dying (of happiness, no doubt) to receiving insurance funds after your death. For example, if you die in a house fire, the company that insures your home may need to pay for damages done to the property. In such case, the funds will need to be paid to your Estate. A Personal Representative may need to be appointed and the insurance funds distributed according to New York law.

If you die without a Will, the Personal Representative may not be the person you would have chosen. The monies may be distributed differently than you would have wished.

And there are other important reasons to make a Will.

ARRANGE FOR PERSONAL REPRESENTATIVE FEES

An important reason to make a Will is to appoint the person of your choice as Personal Representative and to come to an understanding about how much he will be paid to serve in this capacity. If you do not make provision for his fee, then he is entitled to receive the amount as stated under New York law (Surrogates 2307). That fee is substantial. For example, an Estate worth $100,000 will pay $5,000 in commissions to the Personal Representative (see page 22).

 THE PERSONAL REPRESENTATIVE CAN SEEK MORE MONEY

Even though your Personal Representative verbally agrees to charge only a certain amount, he may find the job to be more than he expected and decide to take the statutory amount after all. To avoid the problem, you can have your attorney draft an Agreement with your Personal Representative and attach it to your Will. Having a separate fee Agreement will not stop your Personal Representative from asking for more money, but with such an Agreement, the Court will not agree to the increase unless something unusual occurs (such as a law suit) causing much more work than with an ordinary Probate procedure.

You also need to keep in mind that the Personal Representative's fee is just to administer the Estate. It does not include payment for professional work he may do while administering the Estate. For example, if you appoint your accountant as Personal Representative, he can agree to the amount stated in the Will for his role as Personal Representative, and then ask the Court for additional compensation to prepare your final tax returns, prepare an inventory and do an accounting for the beneficiaries.

The same goes for any other professional, such as your attorney. In fact, if you choose your attorney to serve as your Personal Representative, then under New York law he must disclose to you that he is entitled to be paid as Personal Representative of your Estate and as the attorney for the Estate (Surrogates 2307-a).

A financial planner who serves as Personal Representative may be compensated for his management of the Estate property (buying and selling securities, taking care of rental property, etc.) in addition to his fee to administer the Estate.

If you choose a professional to serve as Personal Representative, have your compensation agreement state what will be paid for duties performed in the administration of the Estate as Personal Representative and what monies will be paid as compensation for any professional service he may perform.

CHOOSE A GUARDIAN FOR YOUR MINOR CHILD

If you have a minor child, you can use your Will to name someone to serve as your child's guardian in the event that you die before the child is grown, and the other parent is unable to care for the child. You can even include a Trust in your Will, naming someone to serve as Trustee to care for property that you leave to your minor child. See Chapter 7 for more information about how to make provision for the care of your minor child in the event of your incapacity or death.

🗐 MAKE GIFTS OF YOUR PERSONAL PROPERTY

Another benefit to making a Will is that you can make provision for who will get your *personal property* (computers, antiques, securities, boats, snowmobiles, etc.). When making a Will consider making provision for your car. If you make a specific gift of your car in your Will, it will be relatively simple for your Personal Representative to transfer the car to your beneficiary. If you do not make a specific gift of your car, then your Personal Representative will decide what to do with it. He may decide to sell it and include the proceeds of the sale in the Estate funds to be distributed as part of the Probate Estate; or he can give the car to one beneficiary of your Estate as part of that beneficiary's share of the Estate.

SMALL GIFTS MATTER

Many who have lost someone close to them report that the distribution of *personal effects* (clothing, books, record collection, radio, etc.) caused the greatest conflict. If you arrange your finances so that no Probate procedure is necessary, then your next of kin need to decide, among themselves, how your personal effects will be distributed. Without guidance from you and no Personal Representative with authority to make decisions, there could be disagreement and hard feelings, over items of little monetary, but much sentimental, value.

If you make a Will, you can include a list of gifts of personal effects in your Will and your Representative will distribute those gifts according to your directions. Of course it is impossible to make a list of every single item you own. You could leave instructions to allow certain of your family members to take their choice of items not mentioned in your Will. You can direct your Personal Representative to use an appropriate lottery system to distribute items requested by two or more family members.

CAUTION YOU CAN'T GIVE WHAT YOU DON'T HAVE

You need to give considerable thought whenever you make a *specific gift* to someone. It could be that you no longer own the item at the time of your death. This could happen with property or money. For example, suppose you leave all of your Estate to you son, with a specific gift of $10,000 to each of your three grandchildren. Your son is the *residuary beneficiary* of the Probate Estate, meaning he gets whatever is left once all of the bills are paid and all of the specific gifts made. If the cost of your last illness leaves your Probate Estate with only $30,000 to distribute, would you want the grandchildren to get their gifts and your son nothing? Of course the simple solution is to make all of them residuary beneficiaries by leaving each a percent of your Estate. For example, instead of making a specific gift to each grandchild you could leave 70% to your son and 10% to each grandchild.

NON-PROBATE ASSETS

You can make provision in your Will only for those items held in your name that do not transfer automatically to a named beneficiary upon your death. For example, property held in a Beneficiary Account, the proceeds of a life insurance policy, Trust property and IRA accounts are all *Non-probate* assets because they will be inherited by your named beneficiary without the need for Probate. You have, in effect, already made a gift of these assets so unless you named your Estate as the beneficiary of these assets, they should not be mentioned in your Will. To do so, might cause your Will to be challenged by whoever was named as the beneficiary of the Non-probate asset.

🗐 MAKE ADJUSTMENT FOR PRIOR GIFTS

With a Will, you can make adjustments for gifts or loans given during your lifetime. For example, if you have loaned money to a family member and do not expect to be repaid, then you can deduct the loan from that person's inheritance. Of course, it may be that you are not concerned with inequities. That was the case of an aged woman with three children, Paul, Rita and Frank her youngest. Frank always seemed to need some assistance from his mother. She often "loaned" him money that he never repaid.

Her other children were responsible and independent. Paul was married and had children of his own. He decided to purchase a house but was having trouble accumulating the down payment. His mother agreed to lend him the money. Paul and his wife offered to give his mother a mortgage on the property. The mother said a simple promissory note from Paul was sufficient, and she would have her attorney draft the note.

The attorney drafted the note but was concerned about the inequity "You never made a Will. Were you to die, each of your children will inherit an equal amount of money. If Paul still owes money on this promissory note, he will either need to pay the balance to your Estate, or have it subtracted from the amount he inherits. But all of the money you gave to Frank will not count towards his inheritance unless he gives you a promissory note, or unless you make some adjustment in a Will (Estates 2-1.5).

"No, it's O.K." replied the woman "I love all my children equally . . . some a little more equal than others."

Most Wills contain an instruction to the Personal Representative to ". . . pay all the expenses of my last illness, funeral expenses, costs of administration, taxes and just debts. . . " This does not present a problem if you are leaving all of your property to one person. That person will pay all of your bills and keep whatever is left. And there is no problem if you are leaving your Estate equally to several people because whatever is left will be distributed equally to those people. But if you leave a specific gift to someone and you owe money on that item, and do not indicate how the loan should be paid, that could create a major problem.

For example, suppose the mother discussed on the previous page, made a Will leaving everything to her three children, equally, with the exception of her car which she left to Frank. Further suppose, that she owed $10,000 on that car at the time of her death. If her Will did not specify that Frank was to be responsible to pay the monies owed on the car, he could demand that the Estate pay the debt. If his siblings refuse to pay the debt, the matter would need to be decided by the Court.

Considering how the mother treated Frank during her lifetime, it is probable that the Court will decide that it was her intent to have the $10,000 paid from the Probate Estate. Should the Court order the Estate to pay the loan, there will be $10,000 less to for the residuary beneficiaries of the Estate to inherit. That means that Paul and Rita's inheritance will be reduced to pay off the car loan, leaving Frank, as before, a little more "equal" than his siblings.

MAKE PROVISION FOR PAYMENT OF TAXES

Taxes are another concern for those Estates large enough to be subject to Estate taxes. State and federal law require that Estate taxes be paid by the beneficiaries of the Estate in proportion to the value received, unless the decedent made some other arrangements to pay for the taxes. If you make no provision for the payment of taxes, whoever inherits your property will pay a percentage of the taxes based on the amount they receive.

The beneficiary must pay his share of Estate taxes regardless of whether he inherits the property through a Non-probate transfer (joint owner, beneficiary of your Trust, beneficiary of a Transfer On Death security, beneficiary of a life insurance policy, etc.) or as the beneficiary of your Probate Estate. If a beneficiary refuses to contribute his share of the taxes, under New York law whoever is required to make payment (usually the surviving spouse or Personal Representative) can ask the Court to order the beneficiary to contribute his share of the taxes (Estates 2-1.8, 12-1.2).

If this is not as you wish you can direct your Personal Representative to pay all of your taxes from your Probate Estate. If you do so, beneficiaries of a specific gift, and those who inherit property from a Non-probate transfer will not contribute to the payment of your taxes. All of your taxes will be paid from your Probate Estate. This means that the amount that your residuary beneficiaries receive will be reduced by the amount of taxes paid.

CAN YOUR WILL BE CHALLENGED?

After reading the past few pages you may think "Looks like everyone should have a Will." And we would agree with your conclusion. Regardless of whether you arrange for all of your property to pass directly without the need for Probate; and regardless of whether you have a Trust, it is important that you have a Will for all of the reasons just stated.

Anyone who is at least 18 years of age and of sound mind and memory can make a Will (Estates 3-1.1). "Sound mind and memory" means that when you made the Will you knew what you were doing (namely making a Will); what property you had and who of your relatives would, under ordinary circumstances, expect to inherit that property.

You may be thinking "That seems simple enough. I think I'll sit down and write one out." But preparing a Will is like figure skating. It is harder than it looks. A Will needs to be clearly worded. A sentence that can be read in two different ways can lead to a dispute over what you intended; and that could lead to a long and expensive Court battle.

Your Will needs to signed according to New York law, i.e., in the presence of at least two witnesses, each of whom, at your request, sign the Will as witnesses. It is important that the Will contain a paragraph signed by the witnesses stating that they saw you sign the Will, and you did so of your own free will and at the time you signed it, you were competent to know what you were doing (Estates 3-2.1).

Neither of your witnesses should be a beneficiary of your Will unless there are two other, independent, disinterested witnesses to your Will. If there are only two witnesses, one of whom is a beneficiary of the Will, then under New York law, the most that beneficiary can get is what they would have received had you died without a Will (Estates 3-3.2).

The problem of having a beneficiary present when you sign your Will is one of **undue influence**. Undue influence occurs whenever someone exerts such pressure on the Will maker so that he is not acting according to his own free will. Undue influence is not easily proven. New York courts have ruled that all the facts and circumstance of the case must be examined ". . . his family relations, the condition of his health and mind, his dependency upon and the subjection to the control of the person supposed to have wielded the influences, the opportunity and disposition of the person to wield it, and the acts and declarations of such person." (*Matter of Anna*, 248 N.Y. 421 (1928), 162 N.E. 473)

Even if the Will is clearly worded, properly signed and witnessed, it can still be challenged if you are married and did not make proper provision for your spouse. As explained on page 43, your spouse has the right to an Elective Share, which in New York, is equal to one-third of your Net Estate, or $50,000, whichever is greater.

Although your spouse has the right to elect against your Will, your adult child has no such statutory right. You can give your child as much, or as little as you wish. You have the right to give the child nothing at all.

If you are concerned that your child, or anyone else, may challenge your Will, it is important that you consult with an attorney who is experienced in Estate Planning. Your attorney can prepare the Will according to your directions and in conformance with New York law. If you meet with the attorney in the privacy of his office, and without anyone else present, it will be difficult to prove that someone was using undue influence to make you give gifts according to their wishes and not yours.

Once the Will is prepared according to your directions your attorney can supervise the signing of your Will. He will see to it that your Will is signed and witnessed in the presence of at least two disinterested witnesses — usually members of his staff. Each witness will sign the Will next to your name as witness; and they will sign a separate paragraph that says, they saw you sign the Will, and you did so of your own free will and at the time you signed it, you were competent to know what you were doing (Estates 3-2.1).

Once signed in this manner it will be difficult for anyone to say that you did not know what you were doing when you signed the Will. If your Will is challenged your attorney will be able to present proof to the Court that the Will was prepared exactly as you wished, and that you had full capacity when you signed the Will.

You can even have your attorney include a *no contest* provision in your Will stating that if your Will is challenged, whoever makes the challenge gets none of your Probate Estate.

Such a "no contest" provision is known as an *In Terrorem Clause* because it is designed to cause fear (if not terror) in the heart of your beneficiary. Many states will not enforce such a clause, because they want people to have the right to challenge a Will, and then let the Court decide whether that challenge is proper.

New York allows the clause, but with a few exceptions. An In Terrorem Clause is not enforceable in New York if:
⇨   there is *probable cause* ** that the Will is a forgery,
     or that it was revoked by a later Will; - or -
⇨   the challenge is made by a guardian on behalf
     of an infant or someone who is incompetent
     (Estates 3-3.5).

This law does not mean that you cannot include an Interrorem Clause in your Will. You can, and if you do, it may discourage frivolous law suits. Anyone who makes the challenge understands that if he loses, there is the chance that the Court will find that there was no good reason for making the challenge the first place. Should the Court reach that conclusion, the Court will uphold the penalty provision and the person who made the challenge will be barred from inheriting anything under your Will. But the challenger also knows that if he wins, the Court must conclude that there was probable cause to bring the law suit. In that case, the In Terrorem Clause will not prevent him from inheriting property under your Will.

** Lawyer talk for "had good reason to do so."

STORING YOUR WILL

Once you sign your Will, you may wonder where to store it. Your attorney may suggest that he place it in his vault for safekeeping. By doing so, he ensures that your heirs will need to contact him as soon as you die. This does not mean that they are required to employ him should a Probate procedure be necessary. It only means that he will have an opportunity for future employment. In exchange, he gives you a good value. Your Will is kept safely in his vault, and at sole cost to him. Before allowing your attorney to store the Will, you need assurance that the attorney will be responsible for the document. You should get a receipt and something in writing that says:

⇨ The attorney accepts full responsibility for the storage of the Will. Should it be lost or damaged, he will replace the document at no cost to you; and if you are deceased, he will, at no cost to your heirs, present sufficient evidence to the Court to accept a valid copy of the Will into Probate.

⇨ There will be no charge to you, or your heirs, for the storage and retrieval of the document.

⇨ Should he sell his practice, retire, or die, he or the successor to his practice, will return the original document to you.

With all of this cost and liability, many attorneys will agree only to store a copy of your Will. In such case, consider storing your Will in a safe deposit box. You can keep the document in a fireproof safe deposit box within your home; and give a duplicate key to the person you have chosen to be your Personal Representative. You might consider placing your document in a safe deposit box that you lease at a bank. The only problem with the bank safe deposit box is convenient access.

THE SAFE DEPOSIT BOX — SAFE BUT . . .

Many people store their Will and other important documents, in a safe deposit box that they lease from a bank or other financial institution. As explained in the last Chapter, if you hold a safe deposit box in your name only, access to the box is restricted once you die. The bank will allow your Personal Representative to enter the box, but if no Probate procedure is necessary, someone will need to get a Court order authorizing the inspection of items contained within the box.

Any member of your family can petition (ask) the judge of the Surrogates' Court for an order authorizing that person to do the following:

⇨ examine the contents of the box in the presence of an officer of the bank

⇨ make an inventory of the contents of the box

⇨ remove the deed to the burial plot

⇨ deliver an insurance policy to the beneficiary named in the policy

⇨ deliver the Will to the clerk of the Surrogate's Court (Surrogate's 2003).

Notice the statute does not allow anything other than the Will, deed to the burial plot and insurance policy to be removed from your safe deposit box, so it may turn out that there may need to be a Probate procedure just to get the rest of the items from the safe deposit box. If you have arranged your finances to avoid Probate, then it is self-defeating to have entry into your safe deposit box trigger a Probate procedure.

LEASE THE BOX JOINTLY WITH ANOTHER

You could lease a safe deposit box jointly with your spouse or a trusted family member. If you want someone to have access to your safe deposit box, but with the understanding that all of the items contained in the box belong to you, then consider giving someone authority to enter your safe deposit box as your agent or "deputy."

Your can give your joint lessee, agent or deputy, the right to freely access and remove any item from your safe deposit box during your lifetime. However, once the bank learns of your death, they will not allow entry to the safe deposit box, not even by your joint lessee. The bank officer can allow your joint lessee, deputy, or agent to inspect the contents of the safe deposit box in the presence of a bank official. The bank will allow a copy to be made of any document that gives instructions for your funeral or burial. This could be a deed to a cemetery plot, or perhaps proof of membership in a burial society. But the only way any other item can be removed from the box after the bank is notified of your death is with written authorization from the Surrogates' Court (Surrogates 2003 (2)).

As explained in Chapter 3, one solution to the problem is to lease the safe deposit box in your capacity as Trustee of your Revocable Living Trust. You can arrange with the bank to have your Successor Trustee have free access to your safe deposit box in the event of your incapacity or death.

I thought you said a Will is not enough

After reading this chapter, you may be thinking that the book is poorly named. After all, look at all the good things a Will can do:

* ✱ choose the person you want to settle your Estate
* ✱ arrange to have your Personal Representative settle your Estate for a reasonable fee
* ✱ give your personal items, including your car, to the person of your choice
* ✱ choose a Guardian for your child
* ✱ discourage a challenge to your Will.

But that is not all there is to an Estate Plan. A Will cares for your property when you are deceased, but it cannot provide for the care of your property in the event you become disabled. A complete Estate Plan provides for the care of your property during your lifetime and for the care of your person as well.

In these days of extended old age, many of us will need assistance with our health care and/or finances as we age. It is important to arrange to have someone manage finances and make medical decisions in the event that we are too aged or too ill to do so ourselves. These topics are covered in Chapters 8 and 9.

And a Will may be effective to transfer all that you own upon your death, but it cannot help your family pay for your debts. It may be that you have so many debts that your family is left with little or nothing. A complete Estate Plan provides for the financial well being of your family once you are deceased; and that is the topic of the next chapter.

Arranging To Pay Bills 5

You can think of your Estate Plan as being composed of two separate parts, a Lifetime Plan and an Inheritance Plan. Your Lifetime Plan concerns the care of your property during your lifetime, with the goal being maximum control and protection. Your Inheritance Plan concerns the inheritance of your property, with the goal being minimum cost and hassle to your beneficiaries. You could consider your Estate Plan to be a master plan that balances the goals of the Lifetime Plan with those of the Inheritance Plan.

When people consider their Inheritance Plan, they are mostly concerned about giving their possessions away. Many do not take into account how the bills they have accumulated will be paid once they are deceased, or even who will be responsible for paying those bills. Most of us do not worry about providing for the payment of our debts, thinking "I'll have that paid off long before I die." But with easily available credit, many are maintaining a high debt balance as a way of life. Paying off all of their loans is not a priority. Many will live their lives without ever being free of debt.

This does not imply that people do not know how to manage their funds. For many people (and corporations), it makes good sense to use other people's money to carry on business. In fact, great debt is a badge of honor for the wealthy. If a bank will lend you a million dollars, it means you have the means to repay that amount. Banks will not lend much money to those with few assets. Rich or poor, we all need to think about how our debts will be paid once we are gone.

Suppose you die without funds, and owing money. Does the debt die with you or is someone else responsible to pay what you owe? If you are married, the first person the creditor will look to, is your spouse. To understand the basis of this expectation, you need to know a bit of the history of our legal system.

Our laws are derived from the English Common Law. Under English Common law, a single woman had the right to own property in her own name and also the right to contract to buy or sell property. When a woman married, her legal identity merged with her spouse. She could not hold property free from her husband's claim or control. She could no longer enter into a contract without her husband's permission.

Once married, a woman became financially dependent on her husband. He, in turn, became legally responsible to provide his wife with basic necessities — food, clothing, shelter and medical services. If anyone provided basic necessities to his wife, then, regardless of whether the husband agreed to be responsible for the debt, he became obliged to pay for them. This law was called the DOCTRINE OF NECESSARIES.

In the United States, a series of Married Women's Rights Acts were passed giving a married woman the right to own property. The New York law gives a married woman the same right to contract, own property and run a business in the same manner as any single woman (General Obligations Law 3-301).

After the Married Woman's Rights laws were passed, cases followed that tested whether the Doctrine of Necessaries still applied. Judges had to decide:

If a wife can own property and contract to pay for her own necessities, should her husband be responsible for such debts in the event she does not have enough money to pay for them?

For those states deciding to continue to hold the husband liable, a second question to be decided was:

If the husband is responsible for his wife's necessities, should she be responsible for his?

Some states decided to make the Doctrine of Necessaries part of their state law. Other states, such as New Jersey, decided to apply the Doctrine equally to both sexes, making the husband responsible to pay for his wife's necessities and the wife responsible to pay for her husband's necessities. Other states abolished the law altogether. For example, in Florida, courts have ruled that the creditor cannot collect from the spouse unless the spouse agreed to pay the debt.

In New York, the Doctrine was not made part of the state law, however New York courts have ruled that if a creditor cannot collect payment for necessities from the debtor, then the creditor can require payment from his or her spouse. (*Our Lady of Lourdes Memorial Hospital, Inc. v. Frey.*, 152 A.D.2d 73, 548 N.Y.S.2d 109 (1989).

Which leads to the next question. Is anyone other than your spouse responsible to pay monies you owe? For joint debts, the answer is "yes."

JOINT DEBTS

A *joint debt* is a debt that two or more people are responsible to pay. Usually the contract or promissory note reads that both parties agree to *joint and several* liability, meaning they both agree to pay the debt, and each of them, individually, agree to be pay the debt. A joint debt can also be in the form of monies owed by one person with payment guaranteed by another person. If the person who owes the money does not pay, then the **guarantor** (the person who guaranteed payment) is responsible to pay the debt.

Should you die, your hospital bills, nursing home bills, funeral expenses, legal fees incurred because of the death are all debts of your Estate. They are not joint debts unless someone guaranteed payment for the monies owed. Hospital and nursing home bills are considered to be necessaries, so if you are married and there are insufficient funds in the Estate to pay for these bills, then your spouse is responsible for payment, regardless of whether your spouse agreed to be jointly liable for the debt.

OTHER JOINT SPOUSAL DEBTS

Your spouse is responsible to pay for loans signed by both of you. For example, if you both are authorized to use a credit card, and there is no money in your Estate, then your spouse must pay the debt. Property taxes are a joint debt if you and your spouse both own the property.

JOINT PROPERTY BUT NO JOINT DEBT

Suppose you have a credit card in your name only, and you have a joint bank account with your son. Should you die, can the credit card company require that half of the joint funds be set aside to pay the debt?

The answer to this question depends on how the joint property is titled. If the account was set up jointly with rights of survivorship, then upon your death, your son will own the account 100%. If you set it up as Tenants-In-Common, then each of you owns half the account. Upon your death, your son still continues to own his half of the account. The credit card company has the right to demand that your half of the account be used to pay your credit card debt. It is important that you verify how any joint account that you own is titled. Under New York law, unless the bank account states otherwise, it is presumed that a deposit account (including CD's) in two or more names, is a Tenancy-In-Common (Estates 6-2.2(a)).

BUT NOT EXEMPT FROM UNCLE SAM

The surviving joint owner of an account has no obligation to use the joint account funds to pay your creditors; however the joint account is included as part of your Taxable Estate, unless the surviving joint owner contributed to the account. In that case the amount contributed is not included in your Estate (IRC 2040a). If Estate taxes are due, the beneficiary of your share of the account needs to pay any part of that tax that is due because of the monies he inherited, unless you make some other provision for the payment of your taxes. For example, you can give instructions in your Will or Trust that all your taxes are to be paid from your Probate Estate or from monies that you set aside for that purpose (Estates 2-1.1, 2-1.8).

PROVIDE FOR CREDIT CARD DEBT

If you hold a credit card jointly with your spouse (or anyone else), you are each equally liable to pay that debt. Should one of you die, the other is responsible to pay the bill regardless of who ran up the bill. If paying that bill could be a struggle for the surviving debtor, you might consider credit card insurance to cover the debt. Many credit card companies offer insurance policies and include the premium as part of the monthly payment. It benefits the credit card company to offer life insurance as part of the credit package, because they are assured of prompt payment should the borrower die.

Of course, in these days of high credit card interest rates, you and your spouse may be struggling to pay your monthly credit charge. Adding still another charge to the account may not be an option, regardless of the security offered to your spouse. In such case, a better route might be for you to remove your name from the account and open a new account in your name only. Your surviving spouse will not be responsible to pay your credit card debts, unless the items you charged were for basic necessities (food, clothing, shelter).

Still another reason not to hold a joint credit card is that each of you can establish your own line of credit. This is especially important if you are married and one of you is retired or has been out of the job market for any period of time. Should the breadwinner die, it may be difficult for the surviving partner to establish credit if he/she has no recent work record. It is easier for the unemployed spouse to establish a line of credit when he/she is married to someone who is working.

OTHER TYPES OF LOAN INSURANCE

Most mortgage companies offer mortgage insurance to their borrowers. Mortgage rates are currently low, so an additional charge for mortgage insurance on the life of the primary wage earner may be worth the effort. This is particularly the case with families raising children. With such insurance, the family can inherit the homestead free of debt. The monthly insurance charge may be a small price to pay to ensure that the children can continue to live in their own home until they are grown.

Car loan insurance is still another thing to consider. If a married couple purchases (or leases) a car, and one of them dies, it may be a struggle for the other to pay off the loan. This was the case with Eva and Howard. Both worked to support their three children. They owned two well used cars. It seemed that one car or the other was always in the shop. When they saw a "NO INTEREST" advertisement for a new car, they decided the offer was too good to pass up.

The monthly payments were high, but it was their only luxury. With both their salaries, they were able to make the payments. When Howard had his first heart attack, he was out of work for several weeks so they struggled to keep the payments current. Howard worked in construction, and was anxious to return to work. The doctors advised that such work might be too strenuous for his weakened heart. Construction work was all Howard knew, and the pay was good, so he ignored the warning and went back to his old job.

The second heart attack was fatal, leaving Eva as the sole means of support for her family.

With Howard gone there was no need for two cars. Eva could not afford the payments on the new car anyway, so she decided to sell it. Unfortunately, what she could get for the car was significantly less than the balance owed. Once she fell behind in payments she decided to surrender the car rather than have them repossess it. She was sure they would understand considering she was a widow with three small children.

They didn't.

The company took the car and then sued for the balance of monies owed. The judge was sympathetic, but under the law there is no "life is tough" defense. He ruled that Eva had to pay the monies owed; and, as per the terms of the loan agreement, she even had to pay the fees for the company's attorney and all court costs. What an emotional and financial nightmare!

The pity was, it all could have been avoided, had they worked payment of debts into their Estate Plan. Howard was the primary driver of the new car and the primary wage earner. All he had to do was to put the loan in his name only, and take out loan insurance. Eva would have inherited the car, debt free. She could have kept it or sold it as she saw fit.

Even if Howard didn't purchase loan insurance, had he put the loan in his name only, the company could only have sued his Estate. They would not have been able to sue Eva personally.

PURCHASING LIFE INSURANCE

The good part of purchasing loan insurance — be it credit card insurance, mortgage insurance or car insurance, is that you can usually purchase the insurance without taking a medical examination. The down side is that companies generally do not offer such insurance to those over the age of 65; and for those under 65 the cost of the insurance is a factor. It usually costs more to purchase loan insurance than a life insurance policy. Those in fairly good health need to comparison shop. If it is your goal to have insurance cover all of your outstanding debts, then the cost of a single life insurance policy may be much less than purchasing several loan insurance policies.

The Estate Planning strategy of purchasing life insurance to pay off all of your loans works best if you are married and your spouse is jointly liable for your debts. If you name your spouse as beneficiary of the life insurance policy, then he/she can use the life insurance funds to pay off all monies owed. If you name your spouse (or anyone else) as beneficiary of your insurance policy, and that person has no legal obligation to pay your debts, then none of your creditors can ask your beneficiary to use the insurance funds to pay your debts (Civil Practice 5205 (c)(2), Insurance Law 3212).

If you want the insurance funds used to pay your debts, then this may not be the way to go. But, if you want to be sure that someone receives money after you are gone, and you do not want those insurance funds reduced by the cost of Probate or to pay off your debts, then this strategy should accomplish your goal.

With or without debt, you may be wondering about life insurance — should you have it? How much is enough? The answer to these questions depends on the "sleep at night" factor, namely how much insurance do you need so that you won't worry about insurance coverage when you go to sleep at night? It is often more an emotional than a financial issue.

Some people have an "every man for himself" attitude and are content to have no life insurance at all. When they die, whatever they have, they have. And that is what their heirs will inherit. Others worry about how their loved ones will manage if they are not around to support them, and decide to purchase enough insurance to maintain their dependents in their accustomed life style.

The same person may have different thoughts about insurance coverage as circumstances change — from no coverage in his bachelor days, to more-than-enough coverage in his child rearing days, to just-enough-to-bury-me in his senior years.

Insurance companies recognize that people's needs change over the years. Many companies offer flexible insurance coverage. As with any consumer item, it is a good idea to shop around before purchasing the insurance.

In addition to the problem of how much life insurance to carry, there is the concern of how the monies will be spent. Leaving a large sum of money to a person who is less than prudent, may lead to a spending spree.

ANNUITIES TO SPREAD THE INHERITANCE

Some people have difficulty accumulating money to leave to their heirs. Some heirs have difficulty hanging on to their inheritance. It is not uncommon for an heir to go through his inheritance within two years. For many, the reason the money is gone so soon, is that there just wasn't much money to inherit in the first place. But for others, it's a spending frenzy. Luckily, people are fairly consistent in their spending habits, so you probably know in advance whether your intended beneficiary will "go wild," or prudently invest the monies he inherits.

If you want to leave an insurance policy benefit to someone you love, but the intended beneficiary is immature, or a born spendthrift, then a simple solution may be to purchase an annuity. An annuity is a type of insurance policy that can be set up so that your beneficiary (the *annuitant*) receives money on a regular basis (monthly, quarterly, etc.), rather than a single life insurance payment when you die.

You can set up the annuity so that it is protected from the creditors of the beneficiary. New York law allows insurance funds paid out as an annuity to be free of beneficiary's creditors (Civil Practice 5205 (c)(2)). For example, suppose you purchase an annuity worth $50,000, to be paid at the rate of $1,000 a month to your son. His creditors cannot force the policy to be liquidated to pay monies he owes.

Of course once your son takes possession of his monthly payment, then those monies become available to pay any debt that he may owe.

As discussed, the beneficiary of an insurance policy inherits the proceeds of the policy free from the claims or your creditors. And that is so, regardless of the value of the life insurance policy and regardless of whether the proceeds are paid out in a single lump sum or whether they are paid out in the form of an annuity (Civil Practice 5205 (c)(2), Insurance Law 3212). And there are other items that are creditor proof under New York law:

✧ THE HOMESTEAD ✧

New York property owned and occupied by a person as his/her main residence is called **homestead** property. The **equity** in the homestead is the current value of the property less monies owed on the property. Up to $10,000 of equity in the property is creditor proof. If there is less than $10,000 equity in the property, then no creditor can force the sale of the property. There are exceptions to this rule. Creditor protection does not extend to delinquent taxes or mortgages on the homestead (Civil Practice 5206).

This homestead exemption continues for homeowner's spouse and minor child — but only until the spouse dies and the homeowner's children have all reached the age of 18. This means that if the home equity is less than $10,000, should the owner of the property die, his creditors cannot force the sale of the homestead while it is occupied by the homeowner's surviving spouse or minor child.

Of course if the deceased homeowner was single, the homestead exemption is lost and a creditor can ask the Probate Court to have the homestead sold in order to pay the decedent's debts.

✧ OTHER EXEMPTIONS FOR THE FAMILY ✧

If a person has his principal residence in New York, then upon his death the following items go to his surviving spouse:

(1)   all household furniture, appliances, computers, musical instruments and furnishings used in and about the house, up to $10,000 in value;

(2)   the family bible, family pictures, video tapes, computer discs, software and books, not exceeding $1,000 in value;

(3)   domestic animals and necessary food for 60 days, farm machinery, one tractor and one lawn tractor, not exceeding $15,000 in value;

(4)   one motor vehicle not exceeding $15,000 in value. The spouse can elect to take cash instead of the decedent's motor vehicle (up to $15,000). If the decedent owned more than one vehicle, then the spouse has his/her choice of motor vehicle. If the vehicle chosen is worth more than $15,000 the spouse must pay the difference to the Estate. If the decedent made a gift of the vehicle in his Will, then the spouse can still chose that vehicle, and the value of the car will be paid to the intended beneficiary.

(5)   money or other personal property not exceeding $15,000 in value, except if there is not enough money to pay for the funeral. In that case the funeral must be paid and the balance of the $15,000 goes to the surviving spouse (Estates 5-3.1).

The value of any of these items do not include monies owed on them, for example if a car is worth $20,000 and there is a loan of $5,000, then the car is worth $15,000.

If the items described in (1) to (4) are not in existence, then no substitutions of money or property can be made.

The five items described on the previous page are called EXEMPT PROPERTY because in a Probate procedure the spouse may ask the Surrogate's Court to exempt these items from the claims of the decedent's creditors — except for monies owed on the item. For example, if money is owed on the car, then the spouse needs to pay off the loan, otherwise the lender is entitled to repossess the car.

If there is no surviving spouse, but the decedent left children under the age of 21, then they are entitled to share the Exempt Property between them. If the decedent was single, with no children under the age of 21, then none of these items are exempt from the claims of creditors (Estates 5-3.1).

✧ FEDERAL RETIREMENT PLANS ✧

Federal retirement plans 401, 402(a)5, 403 (a) (4), 408 A or 408 (d)(3) (IRA and Keogh accounts) are exempt from the claims of creditors. All monies received by beneficiaries of these plans are protected from the decedent's creditors (Civil Practice 5205 (c) (2)).

You may think the above title to be an oxymoron (a contradiction in terms). If a person is bankrupt, why plan for an Estate he doesn't have? But facts are, that people who file for bankruptcy are often quite wealthy and that is their downfall. Because they have substantial income or property, banks and people are willing to lend them money. If more money is borrowed than can be repaid, the unhappy result is bankruptcy. In the event you are concerned about meeting your responsibilities as parent or spouse, yet you enjoy a life style of financial brinksmanship, then consider investing in items that are "creditor proof."

That's exactly what Alan decided to do. Alan was astute, well aware of his strengths and weaknesses. He enjoyed his work and knew he had the capacity to earn large sums of money. But he also knew he was a gambler. Not the Las Vegas type, but a gambler in business ventures. "No risk, no gain" was one his favorite sayings.

If you charted Alan's net worth over the years it would look like the peaks and valleys of the NASDAQ. Lots of high highs and low lows. Unfortunately, he married a woman who did not share his adventurous spirit. His wife became increasingly intolerant of their financial instability. She came to realize that this was his life style and things would never change.

"All gamblers die broke," she said as she walked out the door with their 5 year old daughter in tow.

That, and the fact that he had to declare bankruptcy, brought Alan up short; and he began to be concerned about his future and that of his daughter.

Alan talked things over with his bankruptcy attorney "I am a good businessman, but not a clairvoyant. There was no way to predict the turn of events that led to this situation. But I know I will bounce back, and it will just be a matter of time before I earn my next fortune. I also know that I am an entrepreneur and not a 9 to 5 type guy so this could happen again. What concerns me is how to provide some security for my child in the event that something happens to me before she is grown."

His attorney's response was a surprise.
"Move to another state."

"You're kidding."

"Not really. There are few items in New York that are creditor proof. Other states such as Texas and Florida have greater protection from creditors. For example, in Texas and Florida, your homestead is protected 100% regardless of its value. Only $10,000 of your New York home is protected. As you know from your experience with bankruptcy few of your personal items are exempt from your creditors. But you could put money into a federal retirement plan such as an IRA or Keogh account, and your daughter could inherit that free of your debts."

Alan didn't think that would work. "I am my own boss, and I don't have the self discipline to put money aside each month for my retirement."

Alan asked "What about life insurance?"

The attorney explained "You can purchase a life insurance policy with your daughter as beneficiary. Regardless of the value of the policy, she will inherit the proceeds free of your debts. The only problem with an insurance policy, is that the cash value of the policy is available to your creditors during your lifetime."

Alan was annoyed "You're saying that here in New York, I can protect $10,000 of my homestead, my daughter's educational account and my retirement funds? What about all those millionaires who protect their money in offshore Trusts? If I really hit it big, why can't I do that?"

"You could, but there are many drawbacks. Just to set up an offshore Trust costs tens of thousands of dollars, not to mention how much it would cost just to maintain the Trust."

Alan said "Yes, but if I had millions of dollars that would not be a problem."

"True, but there are other considerations. Once you put your money into the Trust, you are essentially giving up control of that money."

Alan was skeptical "Oh come now. Why would anyone put his money where he can't get to it?"

The attorney explained "The Trust can be set up so that funds are available for whatever the millionaire wants. Usually funds are made available to support his family. Trust funds can be used to maintain the family home or yacht. Monies from the Trust can be used to pay for travel or for an expensive vacation. And of course the Trust would provide for the transfer of the property to the millionaire's beneficiaries, once the millionaire dies. What the millionaire can't do is be the Trustee of the Trust. The millionaire cannot be Trustee, because if he were, he would have control over the money, and his creditors could take legal action here in the United States to force him to use his Trustee powers to use that money to pay his creditors."

"How can they force the issue? Why couldn't he, as Trustee, just refuse?"

"Remember, that as long as the millionaire is a citizen of the United States, and he is physically present in the states, he is subject to the laws of this country. If a creditor goes to Court and wins, the U. S. Judge could order the millionaire, as Trustee, to use Trust funds to pay that debt. If the millionaire-Trustee refused, the Judge could put him in jail for contempt of Court. No, for an offshore Trust to work, the Trust must be a foreign Trust, that is, drafted according to the laws of a foreign country, Trust property must be located outside of the United States, and the Trustee cannot be a citizen of the United States."

Alan said "Well I guess the millionaire might have a relative who is not a U.S. citizen to manage the Trust."

The attorney agreed "Yes, or he could use a financial institution that does not do business in the U.S., to manage the funds. But there are other problems with an offshore Trust. There's the safety factor. Trust funds are kept outside of the United States. If the funds are kept in a foreign bank and the country suffers an economic collapse, then those funds could be lost."

Alan wondered "Isn't that much the same risk as money in a U.S. bank? Only $100,000 of the cash in a U. S. bank account is insured. If the bank fails, any money in that bank over $100,000 could be lost."

The attorney disagreed "Our U.S government is stable, and we trust that they will regulate U.S. banks and keep our money safe. But that is not the case with other small countries. The government of a small country could collapse and the banks along with it."

"But why keep money in a bank? Most millionaires have their funds invested in stocks and bonds, or in real property."

The attorney agreed "True, but real estate could be risky. If your Trust contains real property within the United States, your creditor could go to a U.S. court and take that property."

Alan wondered "Couldn't the creditor take the overseas property as well?"

"He could, but it would be hard. For one thing he would need to find the property. And the Trustee is not about to tell him where it is, unless the creditor sues, and the laws of that foreign country require the Trustee to tell.

The attorney continued "Even if the creditor locates Trust property, whether it is stocks, bonds, or real estate, most offshore Trusts are established in countries that are not creditor friendly. For example, if you set up an off shore Trust in the Cook Islands, they will not accept a judgment that a creditor got in the United States. The creditor will need to employ a Cook Islands attorney to sue you all over again in the Cook Islands. That's expensive. And the Cook Islands have a higher standard of proof. Here in the U.S., all your creditor need do is to show that you owe the money *by a preponderance of the evidence*. That's lawyer talk for "the jury must be more than 50% sure you owe the money." In the Cook Islands, the creditor's attorney must prove you owe the money *beyond a reasonable doubt* (Cook Islands, International Trusts Act of 1984 Section 13B(1)). That standard is the one we use here in the U.S. for criminal cases. In addition, the foreign country usually has a short Statute of Limitations, so if your creditor does not sue you in that country within that period of time, he cannot sue you at all."

Alan said "I can see why offshore Trusts are so popular."

The attorney cautioned "But there are other problems. The U.S. considers transfers into and/or out of the Trust to be taxable. The IRS requires special tax returns to be filed for all foreign Trusts. In addition, the IRS looks closely at offshore Trusts to determine whether they are fraudulent transfers, designed to avoid U.S. income taxes or U.S. Estate taxes. The IRS wants to be sure that the creditor the millionaire is avoiding isn't Uncle Sam!"

Alan said "Yes, but if you pay your taxes, that shouldn't be a problem. If I ever get to the point where I am that wealthy, then we'll come back and discuss setting up an offshore Trust."

The attorney refused "No, I'm just a country lawyer. If you want to go that route, you need a specialist — someone who has overseas connections, and who has experience in writing such Trusts. If you are serious about setting up an offshore Trust, let me know and I will recommend someone to you."

"O.K. I will."

The attorney offered a final word of caution "If you are able to accumulate a significant amount of money, don't risk it all in a business venture. Limit the amount of money you can lose to just the money that you invest in business. Keep your personal funds separate and protected from your business debts. If you want to start a business, make sure that you cannot be personally liable for your business debts. You can avoid personal liability by forming a corporation, or a Limited Partnership, or a Limited Liability Company.** Stay away from a sole proprietorship or a business partnership."

** These topics are discussed in the next chapter.

Your Business Estate Plan   6

It would take a very thick book to do justice to the topic of Business Estate Planning. Estate Planning issues must be discussed for each type of business:

CONTROL	How to control and protect your business during your lifetime.
BENEFICIARY	How to be sure your business goes to beneficiary of your choice.
COST	How to transfer your business to your beneficiary quickly and at lowest cost.

With just one chapter to devote to the topic, we can only provide the reader with an overview of the subject. Hopefully, the overview will give the reader some ideas that can later be pursued with a financial planner, or an attorney.

We have written this chapter for the reader who listed a business value as part of his Net Worth on page 4. People who are self employed, but who do not think of themselves as business owners, may profit from the information covered in this chapter, as well.

This chapter should also be of interest to someone who has the possibility of inheriting a business interest, such as the child of a small business owner, or perhaps the spouse of someone who is self employed. Even those who are thinking of starting a business, may find it worthwhile to take a few minutes to read this chapter.

Those who have no present business interest may want to skip this chapter and go on to Chapter 7.

Your business is your property, and as such it is included as part of your overall Estate Plan. But owning a business isn't as simple as just holding title to a tangible item such as a car or parcel of real estate. For example if you own a business in your name only, i.e. as a *sole proprietor*, there may be no single document that indicates ownership of your business property. You may have filed a Business Certificate with the county and/or state indicating the name of the business and your identity as the owner of the business; but the Certificate does not identify your business property. You could have a truck, computers, copiers or other expensive business equipment. Title to that property is probably in your own personal name.

The business bank account may be in your name only, or in the name of the business with you alone as signatory on the account. Charge cards and business loans are probably in your name only, or your name as guarantor.

If you want to leave your business to your son, how do you do it? Do you leave him the equipment used in the business? If you have a business name that you have not registered, how do you give him that name? And how do you handle business related loans? If you leave him the business, will he agree to be responsible for any outstanding business debt?

Partnerships can be even more complicated, unless there is a written partnership agreement that says how the business is to be transferred in the event that one of the partners dies. Even the transfer of a corporation can be a major headache if there are several shareholders and no shareholder's agreement to say how shares should be transferred in the event of the death or incapacity of the shareholder.

For these reasons, it is important to think about an Estate Plan for your business. You need to ask yourself:

> *How can I have maximum protection and control over my business during my lifetime?*

> *How can I be structure my business so that can be transferred to my choice of beneficiary quickly and at minimum cost?*

We will examine each type of business ownership as it relates to the above questions.

Those who read the first five chapters know us well enough not to expect a definitive answer to the above question. Our job, as we see it, is to explain the rules of the game (i.e., New York law) to the reader. Once you know how things work in New York, you can make an informed decision as to the type of business ownership that best accomplishes your goal.

SOLE PROPRIETORSHIP
Maximum control — Maximum liability

You are the boss if you do business in your name only, but you take full personal responsibility for any loss suffered by the company; and as explained, you may need to consult with an attorney if you want to make arrangements for someone to take over your business should you become incapacitated or die.

Because of this personal liability issue, many people think it best to form a corporation as soon as they start up the business. That may not be the best strategy. It takes money to form a corporation. You may need to pay an attorney to set up the corporation. You will need to pay an organizational tax of at least $10, and $125 to file a Certificate of Incorporation with the New York Department of State. Each year you need to file an annual report with the Division of Corporations and pay an annual filing fee (Bus. Corp. Law 102, 104).

And there may be additional accounting fees. Each year you will need to file separate corporate income tax returns; one for the state and one for the IRS.

You do not need to pay filing fees to the Secretary of State to form a sole proprietorship, and you do not need to file separate income tax returns. You can include your business income as part of your personal income tax return and not go through the cost and hassle of filing a separate corporate return.

Another reason to start business as a sole proprietorship is the risk of failure. Although every new business owner thinks his venture must surely culminate in riches, research conducted by the Brandow Company shows that only 55% of new businesses get to celebrate their third birthday (see their data at **www.brandow.com**). You can always form a corporation should your business succeed. If the business does not succeed, then at least you didn't waste time, effort and money to form a corporation.

But What About My Personal Liability?

Many people seek to limit their personal liability by forming a corporation, however, that doesn't always work in the real world. For example, if you wish to rent a store front or office space, the experienced landlord will allow you to lease the space in the corporate name, but he will require you to sign as a guarantor. That means that should the business fail, he has the right to sue you, personally, for the full value of the lease. Once you have established a successful business, the landlord may agree to just hold the business liable; and in that case having a corporation instead of a sole proprietorship does limit your personal liability.

Regardless of what form of business ownership you choose, you can be held personally liable for any fraudulent or negligent act that you commit. The way to avoid personal liability for fraudulent acts is not to willfully (deliberately) deceive or cheat anyone.

Most of us are honest folk, but negligence is another matter. We all goof. The way to limit your liability for negligence is to purchase insurance that provides protection for mistakes and accidents. For example, if you open a title insurance business, you can purchase an Error and Omissions insurance policy to cover a loss caused by a mistake you might make in a title search. If you have any business involving the care of a person (adult or child day care center, nurse practitioner, etc.), it is important to have coverage for an injury to a client due to accident or malpractice.

If you have a business location (a storefront or office) consider purchasing a comprehensive business insurance policy to cover injury to anyone who visits your business, as well as damages to the premises. For example, if you open a flower shop you can get insurance to cover an injury to a customer who slips and falls. The same policy can cover vandalism to your shop, such as a broken plate glass window. You can be compensated for loss should a storm cause the electricity to go out and your shipment of fresh cut flowers wilt for lack of refrigeration.

The purpose of any business insurance policy is to shift the risk of a business loss from your pocket to that of the insurance company.

And the downside is . . .
The problem with insurance is the greater the risk, the greater the cost. We all would like 100% insurance coverage, but few of us can afford the premium. What holds true for life insurance holds true for business insurance. The right amount of insurance coverage for you is the amount that allows you to sleep at night.

BUSINESS PARTNERSHIP
Shared control — Maximum liability

A business partnership is much like a marriage. You can both start out with the best of intentions, only to find that you are hopelessly incompatible. The break-up of a business partnership can be just as bitter and hotly contested as the breakup of a marriage. A properly drafted Partnership Agreement is a must — not only to set the terms of a dissolution, but to clearly state what is expected of each partner; i.e., how much each will contribute to the business venture in terms of effort or financing.

The Partnership Agreement should cover what will happen to the partner's share in the event of his incapacity or death. Most Partnership Agreements provide for an appraisal of the business and the buy out of the deceased (or disabled) partner's share. The Partnership Agreement may need to be backed up with financing. For example, you could sign a Partnership Agreement that requires the company to buy out your partnership interest should you become disabled or die. But what good is the Agreement if there is not enough cash in the company to pay for the buy out?

You will have better protection if the Partnership Agreement requires the company and/or partners to maintain insurance, and that the proceeds of the policy be used to pay for the buy out. Many insurance companies offer Key man insurance. The policy is designed to compensate the company for the loss of someone who is essential to the continuation of the business. If sufficient insurance is purchased, the proceeds of the policy can be used to cover any loss suffered by the company and to buy out the share of the company that was owned by the deceased or disabled partner.

The sole proprietorship and the partnership are the earliest type of business organization. New York laws governing these types of business organizations have their roots in English Common Law. Common law requires the sole proprietor and each business partner to take full personal responsibility for the debts of the company. As people became ever more litigious (lawyer talk for "sue happy") businessmen sought to limit their liability and prevailed on the legislature to create a form of business ownership to limit that liability.

Legislatures in each state responded to that need by giving businessmen the right to create a company (the corporation) with an identity separate from the owners of the business. By doing business as a corporation, the businessman's liability is limited to the money he invests in the company. A person can sue the corporation for business debts, but not the owners of the corporation.

This does not mean that a corporate owner can use the corporation to do things that are fraudulent. If he does, he can be held personally liable. The owner of the corporation cannot use the corporation as a "veil" to cover his wrongdoing. The Court of Appeals of the State of New York ruled that courts in New York have authority to disregard the corporate form and "pierce the corporate veil" where necessary "to prevent fraud or to achieve equity." (*Int'l Aircraft Trading Co. v. Manufacturers Trust Co.* 297 N.Y. 285, 79 N.E.2d 249 (1948)).

THE CORPORATION
flexible control — limited liability

Whoever forms a corporation (the *incorporator*) has maximum control over the corporation. He decides how the company will operate by having the Articles of Incorporation and the company By-laws prepared according to his specifications. He can keep full control of the company as the only shareholder, or he can distribute shares and give up as much control as he wishes.

Transferring corporate ownership is simple. It is a matter of signing a stock certificate transferring the shares of stock in the company. If you own shares of stock in your name only, then upon your death, your Personal Representative will transfer the shares according to your Will, or if no Will, according to the Rules Governing Intestate Succession. But keeping shares in your name only, may not be the best way to go if you own a majority of shares and operate the business yourself. If Probate is necessary, it may take several months before the shares are transferred to the proper beneficiary, meanwhile, someone needs to continue to operate the business. If you do not leave specific directions for the continuance of the business, the Personal Representative (or the Surrogate's Court) may decide it best to just sell the company and give the proceeds of the sale to your beneficiaries.

The better route is to have your attorney prepare a Revocable Living Trust and transfer the shares into the Trust. The Trust document can give your Successor Trustee specific instructions about how the business is to be managed or transferred should you become incapacitated or die. Still another important benefit is to avoid the need to Probate what may be your only valuable asset.

THE LIMITED PARTNERSHIP

Just as a sole proprietor can limit his liability by forming a corporation, the owners of a business partnership can limit their liability by converting the partnership to a *Limited Partnership*. As with the corporation, the Limited Partnership is a creation of the legislature and is regulated by New York law. The name of the Limited Partnership must identify it as a limited partnership or contain the initials "LP." A Certificate of Limited Partnership must be filed with the New York Department of State (Partnership 121-102, 121-201).

The structure of a Limited Partnership differs from a business partnership. In a business partnership, each partner has full authority to conduct business on behalf of the partnership. Each partner is personally liable for monies owed by the partnership, regardless of whether that partner actually incurred the debt. The Limited Partnership has General Partners and Limited Partners. Only a General Partner of a Limited Partnership has authority to conduct partnership business; and only a General Partner is liable for company debts. A Limited Partner has no control over the management of the company. A Limited Partner has no personal liability for company debts (Partnership 121-303, 121-403).

But even a General Partner can avoid personal liability by forming a corporation, and then letting the corporation serve as the sole General Partner. An unpaid creditor of the Limited Partnership can sue the corporate General Partner, but not the shareholders of the corporation. Liability can be limited to the amount of money invested in the business venture. None of the owners will have personal liability. Of course, as with the corporation, all parties can be held personally liable for fraudulent or criminal acts performed in their partnership capacity.

The astute reader might be wondering "Why form a corporation (and pay all of the monies associated with that corporation) and then make that corporation the general partner of a Limited Partnership (and then pay all of the monies associated with that organization). If limited business liability is the goal, why not just form a corporation?"

The answers to that question are many and in fact, far removed from the original goal of limiting the business risk of the partners to just the monies they invested in the business. The Limited Partnership can be used as a means of transferring a family business to the children with some significant tax benefits. For example, suppose Mom & Pop run a small, highly profitable, rapidly expanding, gourmet chocolate shop. They have two children, both in college. Right now, the business is worth about $500,000, but they figure that by the time they retire, the business could be worth millions. If their children inherit the business at that time, there could be significant Estate Taxes due. Also, because they are making lots of money right now, they are paying very high income taxes.

Both problems can be solved with a Family Limited Partnership. Mom and Pop can be the general partners of the company and retain total control. They could make each child a limited partner by transferring 2% of the company to each child. This gift is worth less than $11,000, so the gift has no Gift Tax consequences. Mom and Pop can continue to gift shares of the partnership each year. By gifting a percentage of the business each year, the parents can essentially transfer all of the business to the children. When the parents die, there will be no Gift or Estate tax because the children already own the business. Of course there is still the problem of the Capital Gains tax should the children decide to sell the business.

Regardless of how much of the company they give away, Mom and Pop can keep total control of the company because they are the general partners. When the parents are ready to retire, one or both of the children can take over as general partner — but if making chocolate is not their thing, the parents can arrange to have a corporation manage the Limited Partnership and the children continue to receive income as limited partners.

As for the current income tax problem, the children, as limited partners, are entitled to receive income from the business. Income paid to the children and their parents is generally taxed at a lower rate than the taxes to just Mom and Pop. For example, suppose the company earns $100,000. Mom and Pop will pay a high rate of income tax if they are the only two partners in the company. If the children become partners, then each partner can earn $25,000 and the overall bill for income taxes will be smaller.

Still another important advantage of the Family Limited Partnership over the corporation is creditor protection for the children's partnership interest. For example, suppose one of the children, becomes a dentist, gets sued for malpractice, and loses the case. If Mom and Pop had incorporated the business and given the children most of the shares of stock in the company, the creditor could take the shares to satisfy the judgment. The creditor could wind up owning the company! Not so, with a Limited Partnership interest. A judge could order that the income from the Limited Partnership be used to pay the judgment, but he could not order the Partnership share itself to be given to the creditor as payment for the debt unless the Limited Partnership Agreement allows for such transfer AND all other partners agree (Partnership 121-703, 121-704). Not likely, with Mom and Pop as general partners. They might even decide to pay all the income to themselves and not distribute any to the hapless creditor!

We used an actual business as an example to explain how the Limited Partnership worked. It didn't take Estate Planning attorneys long to figure out that the "family business" could be just income producing items (such as stocks and bonds) that Mom and Pop placed into the Limited Partnership. The family "business" could be just the business of managing a portfolio. In other words, the Family Limited Partnership could just be a type of an Estate Plan created solely for the purpose of transferring assets to the children to avoid paying Estate Taxes, and to pay less in income taxes.

It didn't take the IRS long to challenge this method of Estate Planning. A series of IRS rulings and court cases followed, with the main issue being whether a bonafide business partnership existed.

There is a common sense rule of evidence that says "If it looks like a duck and walks like a duck, and quacks like a duck, it must be a duck." In 1946 the Supreme Court decided that whether a family partnership is really a business partnership for tax purposes, should be determined on a case by case basis; and that the IRS should use the "walk and quack" test. Only the justices said this in proper legal terms. They said that to determine whether a partnership exists depends on ". . .whether the partners really and truly intended to join together for the purpose of carrying on a business and sharing in the profits or losses or both. And their intention in this respect is a question of fact, to be determined from testimony disclosed by their agreement, considered as a whole, and by their conduct in execution of its provisions" (*Commissioner v. Tower*, 327 U.S. 280 (1946)).

THE LIMITED LIABILITY COMPANY

The IRS continues to take a close look at family partnerships, and will challenge any tax break if the family partnership (limited or not) does not meet the basic requirement of being a bonafide business partnership. Perhaps in response to IRS challenges, in the 1990s each of the 50 states, and even the District of Columbia, passed laws enabling the residents of their state to form a new business entity called a *Limited Liability Company* ("LLC" or "L.L.C.").

This new entity is not required to be a profit making venture. It can be formed to carry on any lawful business. A New York LLC is formed by filing Articles of Organization with the New York Secretary of State (LLC Law 201, 203, 204).

The LLC combines the better features of the Limited Partnership and the Corporation. Like the corporation, it can be formed by a single person who can set the rules of the company when he forms the company. The rules of an LLC are called an *Operating Agreement.* Each member of the LLC must agree to conduct business in accordance with the company's Operating Agreement.

The LLC can be run by a manager who is not a member of the company, or it can be run by a member or members of the company. As with a corporation, all members have limited liability, regardless of whether that member happens to be managing the company. As with a Limited Partnership, a creditor cannot take possession or control of a share of the company owned by a member. The most the creditor can do is get a court to assign income generated by that share to the creditor (LLC Law 603, 609).

Now Mom and Pop can form a LLC, give away some or all of the shares of the company during their lifetime, and still keep control of the company, and with no more personal liability than a non-managing member of the Limited Liability Company.

Transfers into the Limited Liability Company can be made so that there is no Estate or Gift tax issue. Income can be distributed to the children, or not, as Mom and Pop see fit.

The astute reader is probably thinking "Maximum control, limited liability, easily transferred to my heirs, no Estate tax. This is too good to be true. There must be a catch somewhere."

And so there is. It's called the Capital Gains tax. If you transfer property during your lifetime, that property is valued by the IRS as of the date of transfer. If you gift a share of the partnership during your lifetime, your beneficiary will take your basis in the property (i.e., the value that you paid for the partnership interest). If you sell the share to your beneficiary, then his basis is the fair market value of the share as of the date of purchase. Either way, once the beneficiary decides to sell the property, there may be a significant Capital Gains tax due.

An experienced Estate Planning attorney should be able to suggest any number of ways to solve the problem, including purchasing life insurance to pay the tax.

Regardless of what form of business ownership you have, you need to think about what will happen to your business in the event of your incapacity or death. And in particular, how company debts will be paid. If your business is highly leveraged (business talk for "owes lots of money") you also need to consider how those loans will be paid should you become disabled or die. One solution is to purchase key man insurance. A key man insurance policy is a life and disability policy that protects the company against the loss of a valuable employee. The company purchases the policy and the proceeds are paid to the company to compensate it for the loss; but ultimately the policy benefits those who inherit the business.

Taxes are still another concern. Your business may be worth millions on paper, and your Estate Taxes will be based on that value. Your heirs might be forced to sell the company just to pay the taxes, but without your leadership they may get only a fraction of the value of the company.

Even if the federal government decides to eliminate federal Estate Taxes, the state of New York, or any other state where you have a business location, might decide to levy an Estate or Inheritance tax.

And there is still the problem of the Capital Gains tax. No one in Congress is talking about doing away with the Capital Gains tax — and that tax could be sizeable. One solution to the problem of an unknown Estate Tax and/or Capital Gains tax is to purchase life insurance that can be used to pay for any Estate or Capital Gains taxes that may be due upon your death.

That may sound like a good simple solution, but you need to think things through before calling your insurance agent. The first question being:

How much insurance should I purchase?

That is a tough question. If you are in good health, who knows what will happen before you die. Will your business increase in value or go bust? Will the federal government really do away with Estate Taxes or will they do nothing and allow the tax to be reinstated in 2011?

The last question is particularly troublesome. Under today's tax law, if you purchase a life insurance policy, or even control the benefits of the policy, all of the proceeds of the policy will be counted as part of your taxable Estate. You may be buying insurance just to pay more in taxes to Uncle Sam.

You don't need a soothsayer or psychic to solve the problem. A financial planner with access to computer generated models can predict your life expectancy, how much your business will be worth when you retire and even the probability that the economy will require Estate taxes to be reinstated!

Suppose your financial planner predicts that Estate taxes will be reinstated and that your heirs will probably need to pay 1 million dollars. If you purchase a million dollar insurance policy, the value of the policy will be included in your Estate. If there is an Estate Tax of 40% your heirs will net only $600,000 of your million dollar policy, the rest going for Estate taxes on the proceeds of the policy itself.

Your heirs will need to come up with an additional $400,000 to make up for the original million dollars predicted as being necessary to pay your Estate taxes. The solution to this dilemma is the ***Irrevocable Insurance Trust***.

THE IRREVOCABLE INSURANCE TRUST

An Irrevocable Insurance Trust can be designed to provide money to pay any tax that may be due after your death. To be sure that the IRS does not count the proceeds of the Trust as part of your taxable Estate the Trust must meet the following requirements:

⇨   The Trust must be irrevocable.

⇨   Neither you nor your spouse can be Trustee.

The Trust can be set up for the benefit of your child. In such case, the child can be Trustee of the Trust. The child, as Trustee, will purchase an insurance policy on your life. If you give the child a large sum of money to purchase the policy, then you may need to file a gift tax return. It is better to give the child $11,000 a year and have the child purchase a policy that is paid with quarterly or annual premiums instead of a single lump sum payment. If you are married, you and your spouse can gift up to $22,000 per year without the need to file a Gift tax return.

As tax laws change, the child/Trustee can use as much of the gift as is needed to purchase sufficient insurance to cover the taxes. The Trust can be written to cover Estate taxes or Capital Gains taxes, or both. For example, the Trustee can purchase an insurance policy that pays a million dollars upon your death. The Trust document can direct the Trustee to use the proceeds of the insurance policy to pay your Estate taxes. Should it happen that no Estate taxes are due, the Trust can direct the Trustee to keep the monies invested until the business is sold, when the Trust funds can be used to pay any Capital Gains tax that may be due. If monies are left over once all taxes are paid, they can be distributed to the named beneficiaries of the Trust.

Your attorney can design an Irrevocable Insurance Trust in any number of ways to meet the special needs of you and your family. For example, an Irrevocable Insurance Trust can be set up to solve problems described in the last Chapter. Alan wanted to leave insurance proceeds for his child but was concerned that the cash value of the policy could be taken by his creditors. A properly drafted Irrevocable Insurance Trust can solve such problem, because the Trust and not Alan is the owner of the policy.

Of course, it costs significant money to set up and maintain an Irrevocable Insurance Trust. Those who do not have concerns about creditors may wonder whether it's necessary to go through all that cost and bother if there will be no more Estate taxes in the future. After all a simple life insurance policy can cover any Capital Gains tax that may be due. But, as explained, the tax law as passed in 2001 reinstates the Estate Tax in 2011. If lawmakers take no further action, the Estate of anyone who dies on January 1, 2011, and thereafter is subject to an Estate Tax for an Estate over one million dollars.

Someone with an active imagination could envision the following scenario:

It is New Year's eve, 2010. A 97 year old lies sleeping, at his home, surrounded by his four grandchildren who are his sole heirs.

"He looks so peaceful."

"Yes. Surprising, considering that he has terminal cancer, failing kidneys and heart. His doctor says he can't last more than a few days. The doctor left a supply of morphine so that we can keep Gramps comfortable over the New Year's holiday. The doctor gave him a shot just before he left."

"The doctor said not to give Gramps another shot unless he was in pain. His heart is in such a weakened condition, he could easily overdose on morphine."

"Yes, of course."

"Too bad he didn't get a chance to do some Estate Planning before he had that stroke last year. "

"I thought his attorney took care of all that."

"His attorney suggested he set up an Irrevocable Insurance Trust to pay for any Estate Tax, but Gramps felt sure that Congress would pass a law that would permanently repeal the Estate Tax."

"I can't imagine Gramps coming to that conclusion. The economy is down and the government needs to raise taxes. It is easier for legislators to leave the law as written back in 2001, then take some affirmative action."

"Gramps was always an astute business man, but in his later years his mind wasn't as sharp as when he earned his 5 million dollars."

"Is that what we are going to inherit?"

"Not unless he dies before midnight. After midnight the Estate Tax is reinstated, and at a rate of 45%. Between state and federal taxes, we'll be lucky to come away with half a mill each."

"Gramps moved. I think he may be in pain."

"Yes, he does look uncomfortable."

"It isn't right to let him suffer like this."

"Yes, of course."

Continuing To Care 7

There are any number of reasons that people give for wanting to continue on with their lives. For the lucky ones, their main reason for living is that they are having a great time and don't want it to end. For many, it is more a sense of responsibility. During child rearing years the concern of the parent is what will happen to the child should the parent suddenly die. Once a child is grown, the roles often reverse, and it is the child worrying about what will happen to his parent if the child were not present to see to the care of the aging parent. Even pet lovers worry about what will happen to their pet should the owner no longer be around.

There is little that can be done to prepare those who depend on you for the loss of your companionship and emotional support; but there are many things you can do to provide financial support for those who rely on you. Even people of modest means can make financial provision so their loved ones will have an easy transition from being dependent to becoming self sufficient.

This chapter explains the many simple, and relatively inexpensive, things you can do to provide care for your loved ones should you not be present to do so yourself.

PROVIDING FOR THE MINOR CHILD

It doesn't happen very often, but both parents could die or become incapacitated before their child reaches adulthood. Most parents don't want to think about, much less prepare for such a happening. But in this age of postponing parenthood, many parents are raising children into their fifties and sixties. The probability of a life threatening illness increases with age, so parents need to understand the importance of planning ahead.

Parents with dangerous occupations also need to provide for the care of their minor child in event of the disability or death of both parents. It is surprising to think of how many of us are employed in dangerous occupations. Construction workers, military personnel, firemen, state and federal law enforcement agents, and in this day and age, even postal workers face hazards on a daily basis.

Regardless of the parent's age or occupation, planning for the care of a minor child should be part of every parent's Estate Plan, not only because it is the responsible thing to do, but also because it is relatively simple and inexpensive to do.

A child must be cared for in two ways, the **person** of the child and the **property** of the child. To care for the person of the child, someone must be in charge of the child's everyday living, not only food and shelter but to provide social, ethical and religious training. Someone must have legal authority to make medical decisions and see to the child's education. To care for the child's property, someone must be responsible to see that monies left to the child are used for the care of the child and that anything left over is preserved until the child becomes an adult.

APPOINTING A GUARDIAN FOR YOUR CHILD

As a parent, you have the right to name someone in your Will to serve as your child's Guardian. You can appoint someone to serve as the Guardian of the child's person, and another to serve as the Guardian of the child's property, or you can name someone to serve in both capacities (person and property). The surviving parent has the right (and duty) to care for the child, so the Guardian you choose can serve in that capacity only if the other parent is deceased or incapacitated to the point that he/she cannot care for the child.

It is a good idea for both parents to name the same guardian in their respective Wills because if the parents die simultaneously, then a Judge will decide who shall serve as Guardian. And it is important to choose someone who is compatible with the child because if the child is 14 or older, the Court will seriously consider the child's choice of guardian.

The person you name as Guardian needs to know of your Will (and its location) so that he/she can take over should the need arise. You need to explain to the person you appoint as Guardian that he/she is not the legal Guardian until a Judge of the Surrogate's Court makes it official. Upon your death, your Will needs to be filed with the Court so the Judge will know your choice of Guardian. The person you appoint as Guardian has 3 months from your date of death to ask the Probate Court to be appointed as the child's legal Guardian.

If the Will is not submitted to the Court or if the person you named as Guardian does not apply within 3 months after the Will is submitted, the Court may decide to appoint someone else for the job (Domestic Rel. 81, 82; Surrogates 1701, 1706, 1707, 1711).

THE STANDBY GUARDIAN

A parent who faces a debilitating or life threatening illness, can make provision for the care of his minor child. For example, suppose one parent is incapacitated and is concerned for the care of his minor child should something happen to the well parent. The well parent can prepare a Will naming the incapacitated parent and another person to serve as co-guardians of the minor child in the event that the well parent dies. For the appointment to be effective, the ill parent needs to consent by sworn, written statement saying that the consenting parent:

⇨   agrees to the appointment of the Guardian, and

⇨   is motivated solely by the welfare of the child, and

⇨   has not and will not receive anything in return for his consent, and

⇨   understands that he can revoke this consent at any time prior to the death of the other parent by filing a written revocation with the office of the county clerk (Domestic Rel. 81).

If the ill parent is the child's only parent, he may want to appoint a **Standby Guardian** to care for the person and property of his minor child. The parent can do so by signing a DESIGNATION OF STANDBY GUARDIAN (Surrogates 1726). The statutory form of the Designation can be copied at the law library, or it can be downloaded from the Internet.

 NEW YORK STATUTE WEB SITE
http://assembly.state.ny.us/ALIS

The Standby Guardian can take over as soon as he is notified that the parent is unable to care for the child; however within 60 days, the Standby Guardian must petition (ask) the Surrogate's Court to be appointed as the child's legal guardian.

Even healthy parents should consider signing a DESIGNATION OF STANDBY GUARDIAN to appoint a Standby Guardian for their minor child. It is important to do so if the parent is a member of the armed forces or works in any other dangerous occupation.

The DESIGNATION OF STANDBY GUARDIAN is not limited to a minor child. The parent of a mentally retarded or developmentally disabled person can use the Designation to appoint someone to take over should the parent become incapacitated or die. If the child is over 18, and not profoundly handicapped, the child may object to having a guardian. In such case, there will need to be a Court hearing to determine whether the adult child is in need of a guardian of the person or property, or both. It may take considerable time to collect sufficient evidence of the need (or lack of it) for the Court to rule.

The solution to the problem is to have the parent petition the Court to legally appoint a Standby Guardian, and an alternate Standby Guardian to serve in the event that the appointed Standby Guardian cannot serve as Guardian. The Court will hold a hearing on the matter. Any issues concerning the child's need for a Guardian can be settled at that hearing. Once the Standby Guardian is appointed by the Court, should the parent become disabled or die, the Standby Guardian can immediately take over. The Court appointed Standby Guardian must still apply to the Court within 60 days to be appointed as the legal guardian (Surrogates 1757).

As any parent is well aware, it is expensive to raise a child. The person you consider to be the best choice to serve as Guardian might not be able to do so unless you leave sufficient monies to pay for the care of the child. If you have limited finances, consider purchasing a term life insurance policy on your life and/or on the life of the other parent of the child. If you can only afford one policy, insure the life of the parent who contributes most to the support of the child.

Term insurance policies are relatively inexpensive if you limit the term to just that period of time until your child becomes an adult. Some companies offer a combination of term life and disability insurance, in the event that the bread-winner becomes disabled and unable to work. As with any other purchase, it is important to comparison shop to obtain the best price for the coverage.

If you are married, you may want to name your spouse as the beneficiary of the term insurance policy with your child as an alternate beneficiary. Married or single, you can name your child as the primary beneficiary of the policy. A problem with naming a minor child as beneficiary is that the insurance company may refuse to transfer the funds without Court approval. That will certainly be the case if the value of the policy is more than $50,000 and the child is a minor at the time of your death (Estates 7-6.6, 7-6.7). The Court may decide to appoint a person or a Trust company to serve as Guardian of the property. The Guardian of the child's property will be responsible to see that sufficient monies are used for the care of the child and that anything left over is preserved until the child is an adult (Surrogates 1701).

We discussed the ways a parent can control who is appointed to serve as the Guardian of their minor child should both parents be incapacitated or deceased. Guardianship is a necessity in such case. But if at least one of the parents is able to care for the person of the child, it may be wise to avoid the need for the Court to appoint a Guardian of the property. If you leave the child a significant amount of money the Court will appoint a Guardian of that property. Even if the surviving parent is appointed to serve as Guardian, the amount you leave to the child will be reduced by the cost of establishing and maintaining the guardianship.

An attorney must be employed to establish the guardianship. Once appointed, the Guardian has many duties. He must prepare an inventory and file an annual accounting with the Court. The Guardian may need to employ an accountant to assist with the preparation of the inventory and the annual accounting. Depending on the size of the Estate, the Guardian of the property may need to employ a financial advisor to manage the property. Court filing fees, attorney fees, accounting fees, property management fees are all proper charges to the child's guardianship property (Surrogates 1719).

Monies left for the care of the child may be significantly reduced by the cost of caring for the property. This can be avoided by leaving property to the child in such a manner, that will make it unnecessary for the Court to appoint a Guardian of the property of the child. One way to do so is to set up a Trust for the child, but if you have limited finances, then a good alternative is to appoint someone to serve as Custodian of the gift under the *New York Uniform Transfers to Minors Act.*

The New York Uniform Transfers To Minors Act is a law designed to protect a gift made to a minor. It is appropriate to use this law if you want to make your child the beneficiary of your life insurance policy. To do so you need to name someone to be the Custodian of the proceeds of the policy until the child reaches 18.

You can use the Act if you want to make a minor child the beneficiary of your Will. You can name your Personal Representative to serve as Custodian; or you can name a Trust company or other financial institution for the job. Your Will can your gift be given to the Custodian to hold and manage until the child is 18, or if you wish 21. Should you die after the child reaches the given age your Personal Representative will give the gift directly to the child.

You can even use the Uniform Transfers To Minors Act to appoint someone to be Custodian of a gift that you make during your lifetime. For example, if you wish to give a share of a Family Limited Partnership or a share of a close corporation to a minor, you can transfer the security to a family member or even yourself
"as custodian for _____ (name of minor) under the New York Uniform Transfers to Minors Act."

A gift that you make under the Uniform Transfers To Minors Act during your lifetime is irrevocable. Once you transfer the security to the family member, the gift is made, so this method is not appropriate unless you are sure that you want the child to have the shares once he reaches 18 (Estates 7-6.3, 7-6.9, 7-6.11, 7-6.21).

THE CUSTODIAN'S DUTIES

The Custodian can use as much of the gift as he thinks advisable for the benefit of the child. He can pay monies directly to the child, or use the funds for the child's benefit. In making the distribution he is not obliged to take into account that someone else has a duty to support the child — even if he is the child's parent and it is his own responsibility to support the child.

The Custodian can do the opposite and distribute nothing. He can refuse to use any of the monies for the child and just keep the funds invested until the child reaches 18 (21 if that is the age given in the Will). In such case, the child's parent or guardian (or even the child once he is 14) can ask a Court to order that the monies be used for the care of the child. The Judge will determine what is in the child's best interest and then rule on the matter. Hopefully, the Custodian will give a regular accounting to the child's parent or guardian. If not, any member of the child's family, or the child once he/she reaches 14, can ask the Court to order a full accounting of the custodial property (Estates 7-6.14, 7-6.19).

As with any type of Estate Plan, you need to examine all aspects of the transfer to see if there is anything that may be objectionable to you. We already mentioned the problem with making a gift that becomes effective during your lifetime; namely that it is not revocable. There are other things to considered as well:

THE CUSTODIAN'S FEE

The law requires the Custodian to invest and manage the property in a responsible, prudent manner. The Custodian is entitled to be paid for his effort. If the gift is sizeable, his fee can be sizeable. Before appointing a person or a company as Custodian, it is best to come to a written agreement about how the property will be managed and the charge for doing so.

NO GROUP GIFT

A gift under the New York Uniform Transfers To Minors Act can be made to one child, only. The Act cannot be used to make one gift to two children. If you want to make a single gift, such as a gift of real property, to two or more children, then a Trust may be the better way to go (Estates 7-6.10, 7-6.15).

THE COST OF PROBATE

As discussed, you can include a gift to a minor in your Will by naming a Custodian for the gift. But, as with any gift made under a Will, a Probate procedure will be necessary to distribute the gift to the Custodian (or even to the child if he is of age).

If you are trying to avoid Probate, then this may not be the best option. If you wish to make a significant gift, the better choice may be to set up a Revocable Living Trust. You can fund the Trust while you are alive and bypass Probate altogether. You can manage the Trust while you are able. Should you become incapacitated or die before the child is grown your Successor Trustee will take over. You can instruct the Successor Trustee to use his best discretion to either keep the funds invested until the child reaches a certain age; or to use the funds to care for the child.

Which brings us to another problem, namely, a Custodian appointed under the New York Uniform Transfers To Minors Act must distribute the gift on or before the child's 18th birthday, or if the gift is made as part of a Will, then no later than the child's 21st birthday. The gift must be made regardless of whether the child has sufficient maturity to handle the money in a prudent manner. A sizeable gift to an immature beneficiary is not the best Estate Plan.

PROVIDING FOR THE STEPCHILD

Perhaps the reason that the story of Cinderella has such universal appeal is that many stepchildren, at one point or another, feel left out. The law seems to reinforce that perception. Unless a married person makes provision otherwise, a spouse has priority over the child in health matters both before and after death. If a married person is too ill to make medical decisions, the doctors will turn to the spouse for directions. Should a married person die, the decedent's spouse and not the child, has the authority to agree to an autopsy or anatomical gift (Public Health 4210, 4351).

If a married couple hold all property jointly, that property will go to the surviving spouse and not to the child of the deceased parent. This might not be a problem if the surviving spouse is the natural parent of the child. It could be a major problem if the natural parent dies first. The stepchild of the surviving parent may be left with nothing. In such situations, the stepparent comes across as villain, but it is the parent, and not the stepparent, who decides whether the child will inherit property belonging to the parent. Too often the stepchild is left out by default, i.e., the natural parent doesn't give the matter any thought, or perhaps the natural parent is confident that the stepparent will do "what's right."

That was the case with Walter. He always wanted to be a father, so he was pleased when Todd was born just before the first anniversary of Walter's marriage to Nancy. Their twin girls were born just 15 months later. Unfortunately the twins' birth was premature, causing them to have medical and developmental problems. Nancy had her hands full just caring for the three children, so it was up to Walter to support the family.

Walter was up to the job. He was both conscientious and ambitious. He started his own interior decorating business, complete with a retail sales storefront to sell fabrics, and an upholstery shop in the rear of the store. With hard work and long hours, he was able to make a comfortable living. But the strain of raising a family and running a business took its toll, both on him and the marriage. At 40, he felt like an old man.

All that changed when he hired Annie to manage the retail part of his business. Her energy and sunny disposition were just what the business (and Walter) needed.

Walter's divorce from Nancy was amicable. Walter was a loving father who took his responsibilities seriously. He was generous when it came to supporting the children. Walter had only finished high school, and he wanted more for his son. He encouraged Todd to do well in school so that he could go on to college, and maybe become a doctor or lawyer. The twins had developmental problems; but Walter encouraged them to reach their maximum potential. It was his goal to help them become self sufficient.

Annie got along very well with her stepchildren. She had no trouble with Walter's desire to support the children and give them a good start in life. Even though they held all of their money in a joint account, she never questioned any expense made on behalf of the children.

Walter never gave much thought to an Estate Plan. After all, he was healthy, and in the prime of his earning capacity. He often said that he was fortunate to have married two wonderful women. If he had a dark thought, it soon passed, rationalizing that if something happened to him, Annie would take care of the children.

But she didn't.

Walter died in one of those freak accidents. He was trimming the branches from his tree with an electric saw and accidently touched an overhead wire. All he owned was tied up in the business that he held jointly with Annie. Annie felt that she was a major factor in the success of that business. Why should she share any of her hard earned money with Nancy? As for the children, it was Nancy's job to raise them. After all they were Nancy's children, and not Annie's children. If it was a struggle to support the children, then that was Nancy's problem!

A better argument (but one she didn't raise) was that Walter really wanted Annie to inherit everything. If he wanted to provide for his children, he could have done so in any number of different ways, beginning with his marriage to Annie:

✍   He could have insisted on a prenuptial agreement that would have provided for certain funds to be kept separate for the benefit of his children.

✍   He could have signed a partnership agreement with Annie that would have given his share of the business to his children, in the event of his death.

✍   If he didn't want to negotiate with Annie about a prenuptial agreement or a partnership agreement, he could have had his attorney prepare a Trust that would have cared for the children until they were old enough to be on their own.

✍   If nothing else, he could have purchased a life insurance policy with the children as beneficiaries.

THE SECOND MARRIAGE TRUST

Walter's situation is not unique. Second marriages are common place in today's society. Many who are widowed or divorced, remarry. If children are involved, the parent may have divided loyalties. The parent may want to provide income to the child until the child completes his education, and then leave whatever is left of his Estate to his surviving spouse. More often it is the other way around. The parent wants to be sure that the surviving spouse has sufficient income to support his/her current life-style, but once the surviving spouse dies, the parent wants all that remains to go to his children. A properly drafted Trust can provide for the care of a spouse and child in whatever way the Grantor of the Trust thinks best. That was the case with an elderly widower who married a pretty girl less than half his age. Their prenuptial agreement made it clear that all his property would go to his son from his first marriage. Surprisingly, the marriage turned out well. So well that the couple had two daughters.

The husband decided to divide his Estate equally between his three children and to provide for the care of his wife until the youngest child was grown. His attorney suggested a Trust. "You can be Trustee during your lifetime. Once you die, your successor Trustee can immediately distribute one-third of the Trust to your son who is now 55. No sense to keep him waiting. The rest of your money can remain in your Trust. Income from the Trust can be used to support your wife and children until the youngest is 25. Whatever remains in the Trust can be distributed equally between your daughters."

"Good idea" said the elderly gentlemen, with a smile "Just make sure it is revocable during my lifetime. Who knows what adventures I might be up to in the future?"

It isn't just stepchildren who can be left out if no provision is made. Even children from a long-standing marriage can be cut off against the wishes of a parent. A parent may assume that all of their children will be treated equally when both parents are gone, but if all their property is held jointly, the last parent to die is the one who gets to decide "who gets what." Too often, the wishes of the deceased parent are ignored, for example:

THE STRAINED RELATIONSHIP A child may have a close relationship with one parent, and a strained, but tolerable, relationship with the other. Peace in the family is achieved because the parent who is close to the child acts as a buffer. Should the buffer parent die first, the relationship between the surviving parent and the child may fall apart altogether and the child's inheritance be cut off.

THE PARENT WITH DIMINISHED CAPACITY The more common scenario, is that the surviving parent becomes increasingly dependent on one child — either for emotional support, or for physical assistance as the parent ages. The other children may live at a distance, or perhaps they are too involved with their own family to assist. The supporting child may end up with most, if not all, of what was intended for all of the children.

These problems can be avoided by having your attorney prepare a Family Trust. The family assets are placed in the Trust with the parents as co-Trustees. The beneficiaries of the Trust cannot be changed unless both parents agree to the change. Once one parent dies, the Trust becomes irrevocable. The Trust income goes to the surviving parent and once that parent dies, whatever remains in the Trust is distributed in the manner as was agreed by both parents.

The caregiver of someone who is incapacitated, or developmentally disabled needs to, as part of his Estate Plan, provide for the care of the incapacitated person as well as himself. Should the caregiver become disabled or die, someone will need to take over and make medical decisions for the incapacitated person and see to it that he/she is properly housed and fed. We discussed the appointment of a Standby Guardian to care for a developmentally disabled child. The same strategy can be used to care for an adult who is incapacitated because of age or disease.

For example, an aged spouse, caring for his incapacitated spouse, may be concerned about who will care for his ill spouse should he die first. Often a family member will agree to take responsibility for the care of an incapacitated person. But perhaps no one wants the job. If there are large sums of money involved it may be the opposite case, too many people may want to be in control. One family member may want the incapacitated spouse to remain at home with the assistance of a home health care worker. Another may think the best place is an assisted living facility with 24 hour care. The caregiver spouse may be concerned that a tug-of-war will erupt over who should serve as guardian once he dies.

In such case, it is appropriate to have the caregiver petition a Judge of the Surrogate's Court to appoint the caregiver's choice of **Standby Guardian** in the same manner as was described earlier in this chapter.

The caregiver of an incapacitated person can ask the Court to appoint the person of his choice to be a Standby Guardian. Once the Standby Guardian is appointed his duties will not begin until the caregiver becomes incapacitated or dies. Up until that point, the caregiver remains in control and does not give up any of his rights because of the appointment.

The caregiver can ask the Court to appoint a Standby Guardian on his own, but it is best to employ an attorney to present evidence to the Court that it is in the best interest of the incapacitated person to appoint the caregiver's choice of Standby Guardian. And should it be necessary for the Standby Guardian to be appointed as the legal guardian of the incapacitated person, the attorney will be there to help with the appointment.

If the incapacitated person is without sufficient funds to pay for the attorney's fee, there are any number of Legal Services who can assist in setting up the Guardianship (see page xi).

The person appointed as Standby Guardian must be ready and willing to take over should the need arise. It is a good idea to ask the Court to appoint an alternate Standby Guardian in the event that Standby Guardian is unable or unwilling to serve as Guardian. If an alternate is not chosen, and the Standby Guardian cannot serve as legal Guardian, it will be up to the Court to decide who is best suited for the job (Mental Hyg. 81.02).

Government assistance is available to provide medical and custodial care for those who are incapacitated and without the means to care for themselves. Both state and federal government provide assistance with programs such as Social Security disability benefits and medical and custodial nursing care under the Medicaid program. The family often supplements the government program by providing for the incapacitated person's *special needs* or *supplemental needs* such as clothing, hobbies, special education, outings to a movie or a sports event — things that give the incapacitated person some quality of life.

This is not a problem while family members are alive and able to provide for the incapacitated person. The worry is how to continue that care should the provider die To be eligible for government assistance programs the incapacitated person must essentially be without funds. Family members fear that leaving money to the incapacitated in a Will or Trust will disqualify the incapacitated person from receiving government assistance. Understanding this dilemma, the federal government allows a parent, grandparent or legal guardian to set up a Special Needs Trust with the incapacitated person who is under the age of 65 as the beneficiary of the Trust (42 U.S.C. 1396p(d)(4)(A)).

A Trust set up in this manner makes an irrevocable gift to the incapacitated person, only the gift is held in Trust. The federal statute allows the Trustee to use Trust funds to provide for the special needs of the incapacitated; provided that whatever funds remain in the Trust after the incapacitated dies, are used to reimburse the state for monies spent on behalf of the incapacitated person.

This may present a problem to the donor of the Trust funds. If he gives too little, the funds may not last for the lifetime of the incapacitated person. If he gives too much, then there may be a sizeable "donation" to the state as repayment for government benefits provided to the incapacitated person.

Parents of a disabled child may decide to solve the problem, by leaving money to a sibling with verbal instructions to take care of their sibling's special needs once the parents are deceased. The problem with that approach is security. Once the funds are left to the sibling, they become the property of the sibling; and as such are available to the sibling's creditors.

A better approach is to use a Supplemental Needs Trust as authorized by New York Statute to assist those who suffer from severe and chronic, or persistent, disabilities (Estates 7-1.12).

THE NEW YORK SUPPLEMENTAL NEEDS TRUST

The *New York Supplemental Needs Trust* differs from the Medicaid Special Needs Trust in that monies placed in the Trust do not represent a gift to the incapacitated person. The Trustee can use Trust funds for the benefit of the incapacitated person, or not, as the Trustee sees fit. The incapacitated person owns none of the Trust property so any money left in the Trust when the incapacitated person dies can be distributed in any manner that the Grantor of the Trust directs in the Trust document. When properly drafted, no part of the Supplemental Needs Trust is available to reimburse the state for the cost of the care of the incapacitated person.

You can have an attorney set up a Supplemental Needs Trust so that it is operational during your lifetime. You can name a Successor Trustee to take over the management of the Trust in the event of your incapacity or death. You can direct the Successor Trustee to continue to provide for the special needs of the incapacitated person, and after his death to distribute whatever is left to the person of your choice.

If you want to continue caring for the incapacitated person during your lifetime without going through the formality of a Trust you can have your attorney include a Supplemental Needs Trust in your Will. You can have the Trust funded with monies from your Probate Estate. If you wish you can fund the Trust with a insurance policy on your life. You can direct that the insurance funds be given to the Trustee of the Trust to be administered according to the terms of the Supplemental Needs Trust.

 KNOWLEDGE OF ELDER LAW IS A
NECESSARY PREREQUISITE

It is important that the Supplemental Needs Trust be drafted in conformity with both state and federal law, so as not to jeopardize the ability of the incapacitated person to qualify for government benefits. When having a Supplemental Needs Trust drafted it is important to seek the counsel of an attorney who is knowledgeable in these areas of law; i.e., either an Elder Law attorney, or an Estate Planning attorney with experience in Elder Law.

 CARING FOR YOUR PET

A woman died at peace,
leaving her fortune
and care of her cat to her niece.
Alas, the fortune and the cat
Soon disappeared after that.

You could leave money to someone with the understanding that the person will take care of your pet, but the moral of the above limerick, is that just leaving money will not guarantee care for your pet. The better route is to have your attorney prepare a Will that includes specific instructions and funds to provide for the care of your pet. Those with a Trust can include a similar provision as part of the Trust.

A TRUST TO CARE FOR YOUR PET

If you are financially able, you can employ an attorney to set up a Trust for the care of your pet, or you can have the attorney include a Trust provision for your pet in your Will. The person you name as Trustee will be charged with the duty to use Trust funds to pay for the care of your pet. Under New York law the Trust must terminate upon the death of the pet or at the end of 21 years, whichever occurs sooner (which might be a problem for your pet turtle) (Estates 7-6.1).

You need to name a remainder beneficiary (a person or perhaps a charitable organization) to receive whatever remains in the Trust after the pet dies. If you intend the Trustee to also serve as caregiver of your pet, you can ask the remainder beneficiary to regularly check to see that your pet is treated humanely, if not benevolently.

If you don't have the resources to set up a Trust to care for your pet, you can still ask a fellow pet lover to care for the animal. If no one among your circle of family and friends is able to do so, then ask your pet's veterinarian to consider starting an "Orphaned Pet Service" to assist in finding new homes for pets who lose their owners. It is good public relations and a potential source of income. If this is agreeable to the Veterinarian, you can make arrangements in your Will to pay the Vet to care for the pet until a suitable family can be found. This is a more humane approach than the, all too common practice, of putting a pet "to sleep" rather than have the pet suffer the loss of its master. And in at least one case, that reasoning backfired.

Eleanor always had a pet in the house. After her husband died, her two poodles were her constant companions. When Eleanor became ill with cancer, she worried about what would happen to her "buddies" if she died. She finally decided it best to have her family put them to sleep when she died.

Eleanor endured surgery, chemotherapy, radiation therapy, and even some holistic remedies, but she continued to go downhill. Eleanor's family came in to visit her at the hospital to say their last good-byes. She was so ill, she didn't even recognize them. No one thought she could last the day. Because the family was from out of state, and time short, they decided to put the pets to sleep so they need only take care of the funeral arrangements when she died.

To everyone's surprise, Eleanor rallied. She lived two more long, lonely years.

She often said she wished they had put her to sleep instead of her buddies.

THE CHARITABLE TRUST

We explained how a Trust can be set up to care for a pet and whatever left over (the remainder) given to a charitable organization. There are other kinds of charitable trusts that can be set up to benefit the giver as well as the receiver. For example, suppose you own stock which has appreciated substantially over the years. You are happy with the investment. The only downside is that it pays no dividends. That hasn't been a problem in the past when you were working. But now that you wish to retire, you will need additional income. You would like to cash in the stock and invest the funds in something that can supplement your retirement income, but your accountant says that a significant portion of the value of the stock will go to Uncle Sam as payment for the Capital Gains Tax.

By now you know that a clever Estate Planning attorney will have any number of ways to solve the problem. The dialogue with your attorney might go something like this:

ATTORNEY: "Do you have a favorite charity?"

"Yes, why do you ask?"

ATTORNEY: "You can set up a Charitable Remainder Trust and donate the stock to that charity by depositing the stock in the Trust. Charities don't pay taxes, so they can sell the stock, invest it in income producing property and give you an income on the value of your stock for the next 20 years or they could set up an annuity based on your life expectancy, and pay you an income for the rest of your life."

"What's in it for the charity?"

ATTORNEY: "The charity gets whatever is left after paying you the annuity."

"Yes, but suppose I die next year, and my wife is left without the securities and no income."

ATTORNEY: "No problem. If you decide on a 20 year annuity, you can name your wife or any other beneficiary to receive the balance of the annuity. If you have an annuity based on your life expectancy, and if you predecease your spouse, then the income continues until she dies."

"It seems to me that if the annuity is based on my life expectancy AND my wife's life expectancy, there won't be much left for the charity."

ATTORNEY: "How much is left for the charity depends on the value of the gift and the cost of the annuity. The cost of the annuity depends on the combined life expectancy of you and your wife. I think the best way to understand this plan is for you to look at actual numbers. There are any number of ways to set up a Charitable Remainder Trust. I can explain each option to you. For each option, I will give you the cost of setting up the program; the amount of money you will get; and how much money will actually go to your favorite charity. Of course it must be an IRS approved charity. Once you see the numbers you can make an informed decision as to whether you want to sell the stock and pay the Capital Gains Tax, or set up a Charitable Trust and receive an income."

"Good idea."

THE FUTURE OF ESTATE PLANNING

Up till now Estate Planning for the wealthy was all about the Estate Tax. Estate Planning attorneys would spend their time dreaming up different ways to reduce Estate taxes for their wealthy clients. The IRS would spend their time examining and challenging any Estate plan that appeared too innovative. It seems likely that by 2010 the Estate Tax will be a memory. Is the game over?

Hardly. As explained in Chapter 3, instead of paying an Estate Tax, the child who inherits property that has appreciated more than 1.3 million dollars will pay a Capital Gains Tax when he sells the property. In a way, that makes sense. A major criticism of the Estate Tax was that the tax had to be paid within 9 months of the date of death. That created a hardship for those inheriting a small business with a high assessed value but with no cash to pay taxes on that value.

Critics of the Estate Tax often cited the example of the cash poor farm located on valuable land. Once the owner of the farm died, the family would be forced to sell the farm just to pay Estate Taxes. By substituting the Capital Gains tax for the Estate Tax, that problem is eliminated. No Capital Gains Tax need be paid until the beneficiary decides to sell the property. Theoretically, the family farm can now be inherited generation to generation with no tax consequence.

But there are few family farms in today's economy. Future heirs are more likely to inherit highly appreciated real property or securities that they will eventually want to sell. And when they do, they may need to pay a significant federal Capital Gains tax. Any Capital Gains tax levied as a result of inheriting property with a low basis, might have a counterpart in state taxes. It may be that the heir will pay a New York tax on the Capital Gain as well.

The new game for Estate Planning attorneys will be to devise an Estate Plan that will reduce the Capital Gains Tax. The IRS and the New York State Department of Taxation and Finance will, no doubt, enjoy challenging those plans.

One tried (and legal) method of reducing the Capital Gains Tax is the Charitable Remainder Trust as was just discussed. It doesn't take a crystal ball to see that this could well be the basis of future Estate Plans, so we will take a few more pages to describe the pros and cons of the Trust.

THE CHARITABLE REMAINDER ANNUITY TRUST

A **Charitable Remainder Annuity Trust** is a Trust that is established according to the Internal Revenue Code (IRC 664). Charities do not pay taxes, so property donated to the Trust can be sold by the Trustee free of the Capital Gains Tax. Money from the sale is invested so that it provides an income (an *annuity*) to the income beneficiary (the annuitant) for a fixed period of time, say 20 years, or for the annuitant's lifetime as computed by actuarial tables (i.e., estimated life expectancy). The charity receives whatever is left (the *remainder*) after payment of the annuity. How much income the donor will receive and how much the charity will receive, is agreed upon at the time the Trust is set up.

The Trust can be set up in any number of ways depending on the goal of the **donor** (the person making the gift). In the example given on page 133, the goal of the donor was to convert non-income producing property to income producing property without paying a high Capital Gains Tax. A wealthy donor may be more concerned about his child paying a high Capital Gains Tax should the child inherit highly appreciated property.

For example, suppose you bought acreage in upstate New York that appreciated significantly over the years and is now worth 1 million dollars. You have been putting off selling the property because of the Capital Gains Tax. But it has been a burden to you. It produces no income and because the property continues to appreciate, each year you are paying more and more in property taxes. You did not mind the sacrifice because you figured that your son would inherit the property at a step-up in basis. But now with the new tax law, by the time you die, the property may be worth 2 million dollars. He is only allowed a 1.3 million dollar step-up in basis, so your son may need to pay a significant Capital Gains Tax when he sells the property.

Setting up a Charitable Remainder Annuity Trust solves the problem of the Capital Gains Tax. The land is transferred to the Charitable Trust. Charities pay no tax, so the Trustee can sell the land and the full market value of the property will be available for investment.

The Trust could be set up with you receiving an income for life, and your son receiving the annuity after your death. The only problem with this arrangement is that your son is significantly younger than you are. There may not be much left to benefit the charity if they must wait for both of you to die. The solution is to have the annuity based on your life only and then use part of the income that you receive to purchase a 2 million dollar insurance policy on your life with your son as beneficiary. The 2 million dollars is the estimated value of the land that your son would have inherited at your death. But with this arrangement he will inherit the insurance proceeds free of any Capital Gains Tax.

The astute reader (and probably one with an accounting background) will say "Aha, you may have avoided the Capital Gains Tax, but the Estate Tax Exclusion value does not increase to 2 million dollars until the year 2006. The 2 million dollar life insurance policy counts as part of your taxable Estate, so if you die before 2006, your son will pay an Estate Tax! "

And of course our imaginary Clever Attorney has a solution in the form of an Irrevocable Insurance Trust. You can set up an Irrevocable Trust so that the Trust owns the insurance policy and not you. The insurance policy is not included in your taxable Estate, so your son pays no Estate Tax. See the end of Chapter 6 for an explanation of how the Irrevocable Insurance Trust works.

As with any Estate Plan you need to consider the downside, and the Charitable Remainder Annuity Trust is no exception.

☒ ATTORNEY FEES

It may cost significant attorney fees to set up the Trust. Some charities may offer to have their attorney prepare the Trust at no cost to you, or perhaps they offer a "standard" Trust document that their attorney prepared. But, using their Trust document represents a conflict of interest. Their Trust was prepared by an attorney for the greatest benefit to his client (that's the charity, not you). It is important that you employ your own attorney to represent you. He knows the extent of your Estate and he understands what you wish to accomplish.

⊠ THE COMPLEXITY OF THE PLAN

A Charitable Remainder Annuity Trust is a sophisticated Estate Plan designed to benefit the well-to-do donor and an IRS approved charity. There are any number of ways to set up the plan. It is important to have an attorney or financial planner, who will take the time to explore different plans until you determine the best plan for you.

⊠ THE TRUST IS IRREVOCABLE

Once established, the Trust is not revocable, so it is important that you understand all of the aspects of the Trust. In particular, you need to know how much it will cost in attorney's fees to set up the Trust; and how much income you will receive, and over what period of time. The income you receive as an annuitant is taxable to you. You need to consider that while taxes change over the years, the terms of the Trust cannot be changed. It is important that your attorney, accountant or financial planner give you some idea of what you might expect in terms of future income tax payments.

Although future income tax payments may be a question mark, the power of the Charitable Trust is the tax benefit to the donor at the time the Trust is set up.

☑ NO CAPITAL GAINS TAX

Had you sold the property and invested the money yourself, you would have had to pay a Capital Gains Tax and that tax could be substantial, depending on the tax rate in effect at the time of the transfer. By gifting the property the full value of the land can be used to produce investment income.

☑ NO PROPERTY TAX

Once your property is transferred into the Trust, you will no longer need to pay annual property taxes.

☑   NO GIFT TAX

The property you transfer into the Trust is a gift to a charity and as such is not included in the sum total of taxable gifts that you give during your lifetime.

☑   INCOME TAX DEDUCTION

Because you are making a charitable donation, you should be able to take a charitable deduction on your income tax in the year of the donation.

And there are other benefits to setting up a Charitable Trust:

☑   NO PROBATE EXPENSE

It might take an expensive and time consuming Probate procedure to transfer the property to a beneficiary upon your death. By transferring the property to the Trust during your lifetime, you avoid the need for a Probate procedure to transfer the property after your death.

☑   GIVE WHEN NEEDED INSTEAD OF LATER

A Charitable Remainder Annuity Trust can be set up in any number of different ways to accommodate your Estate Plan. For example, if you are not in need of a present income, but expect that you will spend significant sums on your child's education, you can set up a 20 year annuity with your child as the annuitant. This will get the child through college and probably be a great help should the child decide to start a family. Why have the child inherit property in later, high earning years rather than in the early, high expense/low income years?

☑   CREDITOR PROTECTION

If you keep the land and are sued, you could lose it to pay your creditors. If a beneficiary inherits the land, it could be lost to his/her creditors. But once the property is transferred to the Trust, the gift is made. Neither your creditors nor your beneficiary's creditors can gain access to the Trust funds. The most a creditor can do is seek payment from the money that is received as an income.

☑   GOOD DEED

If you are concerned that your son will be tagged with a Capital Gains Tax once you die, it means that your property has appreciated more than 1.3 million dollars, and you are fortunate indeed. By setting up a Charitable Trust, you are making a donation to the charity of your choice. You are sharing your good fortune with others. You can consider this as "giving back" to the community, or just plain doing a good deed.

BECOME A PHILANTHROPIST

Instead of giving the property to an established charity, you can become a philanthropist and set up your own private IRS approved Charitable foundation. You can be the Trustee of the Charitable Remainder Annuity Trust and your child as Successor Trustee. The Trust can be set up according to your specific charitable purposes. You can use the money to benefit a single cause or several worthy projects. This can be an exciting adventure for those with ample resources and a community spirit.

An Estate Plan For Your Person 8

The law makes a distinction between your property (what you own) and your person (your body). We have been discussing how to set up an Estate Plan for your property with the goal of maximum control over your Estate during your lifetime, and minimum cost and hassle to your heirs once you die. An Estate Plan for your person is just as important as an Estate Plan for your property. The goals are much the same. Maximum control over your person during your lifetime. Minimum cost and hassle to your family for your final disposition.

You may think it strange to speak of planning for maximum control of your person during your lifetime. After all it's your body. Who else but you has any right to control what you do with your body?

That may be true so long as you have capacity, but should you take seriously ill, you may be unable to express your wishes about the care you wish to receive. If you do not have an Estate Plan in place for your person, then your next of kin, or maybe the state of New York may need to make health decisions for you.

The same applies for the final disposition of your body. If you don't make some Preneed arrangements, then someone else will make those decisions for you.

As this chapter will show, it is relatively simple and inexpensive to set up an Estate Plan for your person. You can achieve your goal of maximum control of your person during your lifetime by giving specific written directions relating to your medical care. And in particular, your written directions should include the kind of medical treatment you do (or do not) want to be given in the event you become seriously ill, with no hope of recovery.

You can legally appoint someone to be your **Health Care Agent** to make your medical decisions in the event that you are too ill to speak for yourself. You can give your Agent written instructions about the use of life support systems, autopsies and anatomical gifts. You can authorize your Agent to act on your behalf and see to it that your written instructions are carried out. We will discuss how you can appoint your Health Care Agent later in the chapter.

You can achieve maximum control of the final disposition of your body by making your own burial and funeral arrangements. You can make Preneed arrangements to be buried in the manner you wish and where you wish. If you make such arrangements, there should be no expense to your family for your funeral and burial, and it should be easy for them to complete the arrangements that you have made.

MAKING BURIAL ARRANGEMENTS

Many people have access to a family burial site. But it may happen that deceased family members come to occupy the site, and the rest of the family lose track of the number of spaces left. If this is the case with your family, then you need to take inventory of the number of spaces available and who in the family expects to use those spaces. It is important to contact the cemetery and let them know the identity of the intended occupant of the site.

It may be that the family burial site is not in the state of New York. In such case, it is important to consider the cost of transporting the body from New York to the out of state cemetery. That cost can be substantial, in some cases doubling the cost of the burial. If there is no emotional attachment to the out of state burial site, you may want to consider assigning the burial site to a family member who lives closer to the site and making your own burial arrangements here in New York.

ARRANGING FOR CREMATION

Increasingly people are opting for cremation. The reasons for choosing cremation are varied, but for the majority, it is a matter of finances. The cost of cremation is approximately one-sixth that of an ordinary funeral and burial. A major saving is the cost of the casket. A casket is not necessary for the cremation. An alternate container of fiberboard or similar materials, can be used to transport the body. Embalming is not necessary either, unless there is to be a funeral with a viewing.

Federal law prohibits a funeral director from saying that a casket or embalming is necessary for a direct (i.e., immediate) cremation (16 Code of Federal Regulations 453.3 (b)(1)(ii)).

For those who are considering cremation, there are a few things to consider.

THE OVERWEIGHT

Cremation may not be an option for those who weigh more than 300 pounds. Many cremation services do not have the facilities to handle a large body. If you weigh more than 300 pounds, you need to check with your local cremation service to determine whether this will be a problem.

THE PACEMAKER

Cremating a body with a pacemaker or any radiation producing device can cause damage to the cremation chamber and/or to the person performing the cremation. If you have such an electronic aid, it will need to be removed prior to the cremation. You might check with the cremation service to determine the cost of having the pacemaker removed. Incidentally, a pacemaker can be donated for use in animals with a medical need for the device. If you are interested in making such donation, you can ask you local veterinarian to refer you to an animal clinic that performs the procedure, and then tell your family that you wish to make the donation.

WHAT TO DO WITH THE ASHES

In addition to planning for the procedure, you need to give your family some guidance as to where to place the ashes. Some cemeteries allow an urn containing the cremated remains of a family member to be placed in an occupied family plot. Similarly, some cemeteries will allow the cremated remains to be placed in the space in a mausoleum that is currently occupied by a member of the decedent's family. If you intend to be cremated and all your family spaces are occupied, you may want to call the cemetery and ask them to explain their policy as it relates to the burial of urns in occupied sites.

If burial in the family site is not an option, you will need to arrange for a separate burial space. Many cemeteries have a separate building called a ***columbarium***, which is especially designed to store urns. You can purchase a storage place for the urn in the same manner as the purchase of a burial space in a cemetery. If you wish to have your cremated remains scattered, then you need to let your next of kin know where and how this is to be done.

THE MILITARY BURIAL

If you are an honorably discharged veteran or the spouse of the veteran, you have the right to be buried in a Veterans National Cemetery. If your Veteran spouse was buried in a Veterans National Cemetery, you have the right to be buried in that same grave site unless soil conditions require a separate grave site. You can get information about burial at a Veterans National Cemetery by calling the Veteran's Administration at (800) 827-1000, or visiting their Web site.

VA CEMETERY WEB SITE
http://www.cem.va.gov

You cannot reserve a grave site in advance, so your family will need to make arrangements and establish your eligibility to be buried in a Veterans National Cemetery. At that time, they will need to provide the following information:

➤ your rank, serial, social security and VA claim numbers

➤ the branch of service in which you served; the date and place of your entry into and separation from the service

➤ a copy of your official military discharge document bearing an official seal or a DD 214 form;

so you need to make this information available to the person who will see to your burial.

THE PRENEED PLAN

Consider purchasing a Preneed funeral plan in addition to arranging a burial space. It will be easier on your family emotionally and financially if you make your own funeral arrangements. If you do not have sufficient cash on hand for the kind of funeral you desire, then many funeral directors offer an installment payment plan.

Once you decide on a plan, the funeral director will present you with a contract. The print may be small, but it is worth your effort to read it before signing. If the contract is written in "legalese," then either consult with your attorney before signing it or ask as many questions of the funeral director as is necessary to make the terms of the contract clear to you.

If you are not satisfied with the way a certain section of the contract is written, then add an addendum to the contract that explains, in plain English, your understanding of that passage. If you are concerned about something that is not mentioned in the contract, then insist that the contract be amended to include that item. In particular, check to see whether the contract answers the following questions.

Does the contract cover all costs?
The contract should contain an itemized list stating exactly what goods and services are included in the sales price. Ask the funeral director whether there will be any additional burial or funeral costs such as printing an obituary, or purchasing copies of the death certificate. If you have not purchased a burial spoace, then that cost needs to be factored in. If you made provision for a burial space, then you need to let the funeral director know where you have arranged to be buried.

Is the price guaranteed?

Some Preneed funeral plans have a fixed price for the goods and services you chose. Such contracts guarantee that the goods and services purchased or items of the same style and quality will be provided upon your death, regardless of when you die. If the price for the goods and services that you have chosen under the Preneed funeral contract is not fixed, then the company can charge additional monies upon your death. In these days of an ever increasing life expectancy, it is important that such a contract clearly state how the price will be determined when the contract is finally put into effect.

How are your contract funds protected?

New York laws are designed to protect the purchaser of a Preneed funeral plan. Funeral firms are required to protect funds paid by the consumer of a Preneed funeral plan by placing the funds in an interest bearing trust account within 10 days of receipt. The funeral firm is required to notify the purchaser, in writing, within 30 days, that the funds have been deposited and the location of the bank. Each year, the funeral firm must give the purchaser a statement of the location of the account and the annual interest earned on that account (General Business 453).

Should the funeral firm go out of business, then the firm must, within 30 days, repay all of the monies, together with the earned interest. If the firm is sold, then the new owner must notify the purchaser of the sale, and of the location and amount in the trust account (Public Health 3442).

Laws have a tendency to change. These same laws may not be in effect when it comes time to use the plan, so it is important that your contract states these provisions. If the law is repealed in the future, the funeral establishment is still bound by the terms of your agreement.

Can you cancel the contract?

New York statute gives the purchaser of a Preneed funeral plan the right to cancel the entire contract at any time and receive a full refund together with any interest earned on the trust account (General Business 453 (2)). Because you are entitled to receive the interest from the Trust account, it is considered income to you. Each year you will need to include that interest income on your tax return.

IRREVOCABLE PRE-NEED FUNERAL AGREEMENT FOR THOSE ON PUBLIC ASSISTANCE

People who are applying for Medicaid, Supplemental Security Income ("SSI") or other public assistance programs have limits on the amount of assets that they own. If someone purchases a Preneed funeral plan, then the monies paid into the plan count as an asset because the purchaser of the plan can revoke the contract and get his money back. Understanding the problem, the New York legislature made provision allowing an applicant to pay for his plan by setting up an Irrevocable Trust. If you are in the process of applying for a public assistance program, then before finalizing your funeral plan, it is prudent to check with your local Department of Social Services to be sure that the plan conforms to New York law and will not affect your ability to qualify for the program.

Suppose you die in another state or country?

Your contract should spell out what provision will be made in the event that you move to another state or die in another state or country. Many funeral firms are part of a national funeral service corporation with funeral firms located throughout the United States. You may be able to have the contract provide that there will be no additional charge if the contract is performed by one of the funeral firms owned by the parent company.

Is the funeral firm reputable?

All these precautions don't do much good if you are not dealing with a reputable company. It is important to take the time to check up on whoever is selling you the contract. You can call the New York Bureau of Funeral Directing at (518) 402-0785 and learn whether the funeral home is properly licensed. You may also want to ask how long they have been in business and whether any complaints have been filed against them.

Can the plan be changed after your death?

It may happen that your heirs need to cancel the plan after your death because:

➤   your body is missing or cannot be recovered, or

➤   you were buried by another facility because no one knew that you had a Preneed funeral plan, or

➤   you died in another country and were buried there.

Or perhaps your heirs decide on a plan different than the one you purchased. Funeral firms generally allow heirs to make changes to the plan you paid for such as:

➤   purchasing a more expensive plan and paying the difference

➤   changing to a lesser plan and receiving a refund.

You need to check to see that your contract addresses these issues.

You may wonder why anyone would think of changing the decedent's funeral plan, but consider that in today's market, it is not uncommon for a Preneed funeral plan to cost several thousand dollars. A top end funeral complete with solid bronze casket can cost upwards of $40,000.

And there may be other motivations. Consider the case of Mona, a difficult woman with a personality that can only be described as "sour." Her husband deserted her after four years of marriage leaving her to raise their son, Lester, by herself. Once Lester was grown, Mona made it clear to him that she had done her job and now he was on his own. Lester could have used some help. He married and had three children. One of his children suffered with asthma and it was a constant struggle to keep up with the medical bills.

Mona believed in being good to herself. She did not intend to, nor did she, leave much money when she died. She knew that Lester would not be able to afford a "proper" burial for her, so she purchased a Preneed funeral plan and paid close to $18,000 for it. She was pleased when the funeral director told her that the monies would be kept safely in a Trust account until the time they were needed.

Lester was not familiar with New York law, so when Mona died he asked an attorney at the Legal Aid office to determine whether the Preneed contract was revocable.

It was.

You know the ending to this story.

You may be thinking "All this contract stuff is giving me a headache. Who cares what kind of burial I have? Not me. Why can't I just set aside some money and let my kids figure it out?"

The problem with that approach is that the cost of your final illness may leave you with little or no funds for your burial. To avoid the problem, you could purchase a life insurance policy to fund your funeral and burial, naming one or two trusted family members as the beneficiary of the policy. It is important that the person who is to receive the insurance funds clearly understands why he/she is named as beneficiary of the policy. It is equally important that the beneficiary agree to use the monies for the intended purpose.

It isn't so much that a family member is not trustworthy as it is that they may not understand what you intended — especially in those cases where other funds are available to pay for the funeral. Too often insurance funds are left to a child who then refuses to contribute to the cost of the funeral saying in effect "Dad wanted me to have this money — that's why he left it to me."

To avoid a misunderstanding, put it in writing. It need not be a formal contract. It could be something as simple as a letter to the insurance beneficiary, with copies to your next of kin. The next page contains a sample letter.

> *Dear Paul,*
>
> *I purchased a $20,000 insurance policy today naming you as beneficiary of the policy. As we discussed this money is to be used to pay for the following:*
> - *my funeral and grave site*
> - *my headstone*
> - *perpetual care for my grave*
> - *airfare for each of my grandchildren to attend the funeral*
> - *dinner for the family after the wake*
> - *lunch for the family after the funeral*
>
> *If there is any money left over, please accept it as my thanks for all the effort spent on my behalf.*
> *Love,*
> *Dad*
> *P.S. I am sending a copy of this letter to your brother so that he will know that all arrangements have been made.*

Whether or not you arrange to pay for your burial or funeral, you need to let your next of kin know your feelings about the burial procedure. If you wish to have a religious service, let your family know the type of service and where it is to be held. Let the family know where you wish to be buried, or if you intend to be cremated, where to place the ashes.

Without specific instructions from you, your next of kin will decide and then authorize the disposition of your remains, and that includes decisions about autopsies and anatomical gifts.

THE AUTOPSY

You should also let your family know your feelings about an autopsy. An autopsy is one of those things that most of us do not think about; reasoning that if it is needed, it will be carried out and, being dead, you will have no choice in the matter. But there are many times when an autopsy is optional. Sometimes a doctor is not sure of the cause of death, and asks the family to allow an autopsy. It is often in the family's best interest to consent to the autopsy. The examination might reveal a genetic disorder, that could be treated if it later appears in another family member. Death from a car "accident" could have been a heart attack at the wheel. Perhaps the patient who died suddenly in a hospital was misdiagnosed. The nursing home resident could have died from negligence and not old age. Even if none of these are found, knowing the cause of death with certainty is better than not knowing.

If the death occurred under questionable circumstances your family can request that the County conduct the autopsy. If the County agrees, then there will be no charge to your Estate. However, if that is not an option, whoever authorizes the procedure must agree to pay for the autopsy because the cost is not covered under most health insurance plans.

Many times the family will not agree to the procedure because of the cost. An autopsy can cost anywhere from several hundred to several thousand dollars. Still another reason family members hesitate to allow the procedure is that they do not know how the decedent would have felt about the examination. If you have strong feelings one way or another, then it is important to let your family know whether you would want an optional autopsy.

ANATOMICAL GIFTS

If you wish to make an anatomical gift you can include it as part of your Will; but it may be some time before your Will is located after your death. The better route is to make the donation by a separate writing. You can complete a organ donor card when you apply for your New York driver's license. The Department of Motor Vehicles will provide you with the form and they will indicate, on your driver's license, that you have signed a donor card (Vehicle & Traffic 504).

If you do not want the fact that you are an organ donor indicated on your driver's licence, you can sign a donor card and give it to a trusted family member. You can get a copy of the donor card from your local Department of Motor Vehicles.

If you are well advanced in years, doctors will probably not consider your body for transplantation of body parts, but you can still donate your body for education and research. If you wish to make such as donation you can call the Anatomical Department of the nearest medical school or dental school. They will send you information about making the donation. As part of your investigation, you need to determine the cost and procedure involved in transporting your body to the school.

The cost of transportation to the school of your choice could be substantial if you happen to die far from home. You need to let your next of kin know. If you have registered to make an anatomical gift, then give your family instructions about what to do in the event you die far from home.

If you do not wish to make an anatomical gift, then let your family know how you feel. If you do not make provision for a gift, and do not tell anyone how you feel about donating any or all of your body, then the decision will be up to your family. New York statute (Public Health 4351 (4)) establishes an order of priority to authorize the donation:

    1st   spouse
    2nd son or daughter who is 18 or older
    3rd either parent
    4th brother or sister who is 18 or older
    5th guardian who was appointed before death

If permission is obtained from a family member and there are others in the same or a higher priority, then an effort must be made to contact those people and make them aware of the proposed gift. For example, if the sister of the decedent agrees to the gift (4th in priority) and the decedent had an adult child (2nd in priority), then the child needs to be made aware of the gift.

No gift can be made if the child objects. Similarly, the statute prohibits the gift if the decedent ever expressed his opposition to a donation.

Of course, there are problems with just telling someone how you feel about your burial arrangements, autopsies, and anatomical gifts.

YOU TELL THE WRONG PERSON

The person you confide in may not be present when the arrangements are being made; or you may tell someone who does not have authority to carry out your wishes.

That was the case with John. Once his wife died, he moved to a retirement community where he lived for many years until he died.

John had two son who lived in different states. He would see them once or twice a year. Although he loved his sons, he had difficulty talking to either of them about serious matters. It was easier for him to talk with his friends in the retirement community. They often spoke about dying and how they felt about different burial arrangements. John told them of his young years growing up in a rural community in the plains state of Kansas. "I was happy and free. Out there you had room to breathe. It would be nice to be buried there — peaceful and spacious."

When he died, his friends told his sons about their father's desire to be buried in Kansas. They met the suggestion with scepticism and pragmatism:

"Dad didn't say anything like that to me."

"It would cost us double, if we had to arrange for burial in another state. I'm sure he didn't have that kind of expense in mind."

THE PERSON DOES NOT CARRY OUT YOUR WISHES
Sometimes the person you tell about the disposition of your body may not understand what you said or perhaps they hear only what they want to hear. Whether they follow your burial instructions or authorize an anatomical gift or an autopsy may depend more about what costs are involved, and their own feelings, rather than what you may have wanted.

Even if you tell someone and trust that person to carry out your wishes, it could be that the person you confide in cannot carry out your instructions. For example, if you tell your spouse what arrangements to make, he/she may become incapacitated or die before you do; or perhaps you both die together in a natural disaster or in a plane crash.

WHO WANTS TO TALK ABOUT IT?

The main problem with telling someone what to do when you die is talking about your death. For most of us it is an uncomfortable, if not unpleasant, subject to bring up, and to discuss with those we love. For many, it may be easier to write out directions about the disposition of his body and keep the directions together with other important papers. The only problem with that arrangement, is that people may not find your directions till well after the burial.

The solution to the problem is to appoint someone, a HEALTH CARE AGENT, to carry out your directions about the disposition of your body. You can do so by signing a document called a HEALTH CARE PROXY.

You can use the Health Care Proxy to make arrangements for the disposition of your body. More importantly you can give your Health Care Agent authority to make decisions about your health care during your lifetime in the event that you are too ill to do so yourself.

You can legally appoint someone to carry out your wishes relating to the care of your person, both before and after death, by signing a document called a **Health Care Proxy**. The proxy appoints a Health Care Agent to make your medical decisions in the event that you are too ill to speak for yourself. For the Health Care Proxy to be legally binding, you need to sign it as directed in the statute, namely in the presence of two witnesses, neither of whom are the person you are appointing as your Health Care Agent.

In addition to a Health Care Proxy can sign a **Living Will** i.e., a statement that you do (or do not) wish life support systems to be used in the event that you are dying and there is no hope for your recovery. In the event that you terminally ill and too ill to speak for yourself, your Health Care Agent can authorize your health care treatment in accordance with the directions you gave in your Living Will.

You can have your attorney prepare a Health Care Proxy to meet your special needs or you can prepare your own Proxy using the statutory form (Public Health 2981 (5)). You can look up the statute by going to the nearest courthouse law library. You can also download the statutory form of the Health Care Proxy from the Internet.

 NEW YORK STATUTE WEB SITE
http://assembly.state.ny.us/ALIS

You can use the statutory forms as a basis and then add any provision you wish relating to autopsies, anatomical gifts and funeral arrangements.

USING THE PROXY FOR ANATOMICAL GIFTS

If you want to make an anatomical gift, you can give your Health Care Agent authority to consent to the gift on your behalf. If you do not wish to make an anatomical gift, then you can direct your Health Care Agent not to allow the procedure. Similarly, you can authorize an autopsy, or you can direct your Agent to refuse the procedure, provided the autopsy is optional.

USING THE DIRECTIVE FOR FINAL DISPOSITION

It is also important to include directions for your final disposition in your Health Care Proxy. Your Health Care Agent will have authority to carry out your written instructions. If you made Preneed arrangements, then you should make that fact known to your Agent. It is helpful if you give a copy of your contract to your Health Care Agent.

Some people use their Will to give directions for their final disposition; however, your Will may not be located for several days after your death; long after the burial or cremation. Even if the Will is readily available, the final disposition provision might be challenged once you are deceased. That was the case with the Ted Williams dispute. The better place for those directions is in a Health Care Proxy. The Health Care Proxy is signed and becomes operational during your lifetime, so there should be no question as to what you want, both before and after your death.

Some readers may be thinking "I'm no Ted Williams. My family will surely respect my wishes as to my final disposition. Why bother with a Health Care Proxy? I probably will never need anyone to assist me. And even if I did, my family will tell the doctor what I want."

But, if you do not appoint someone to be your Health Care Agent and give that person authority to act in accordance with your Health Care Proxy, then the person with authority to direct your medical treatment is determined by New York law.

THE DO-NOT-RESUSCITATE ORDER

The **Do-Not-Resuscitate Order** is an order given by a physician directing the hospital staff not to attempt to revive the patient in the event that the patient's heart stops beating. Under New York law the order may be given only in situations where the patient is terminally ill and such medical procedures would only serve to prolong the dying process. Before giving the order the physician must consult with another physician and they both agree, in writing, that efforts to resuscitate the patient would be futile. They must also get the permission from the patient or his Health Care Agent to issue the order.

If the patient did not appoint a Health Care Agent, then they will seek permission from those in the following order of priority :

      1st   a court appointed guardian, if any
      2nd   the spouse
      3rd   a child who is 18 or older
      4th   a parent
      5th   a brother or sister who is 18 or older
      6th   a close friend

A person with priority must be reasonably available, willing and competent to act. If not, the next one with priority will make the decision (Public Health 2965). If this order of priority is not as you wish, or if there is someone you wish to exclude altogether from making your health care decisions, then it is important to sign a Health Care Proxy and appoint the person of your choice to act as your Health Care Agent. If not, life decisions made for you, may not be as you would have wished.

George is a case in point. He was a wealthy man, who was meticulous when it came to his business affairs, but not about his health care. He had his attorney prepare a comprehensive Trust to make sure that his property would be transferred quickly and at little cost to his two sons. His attorney advised "You have made good provision for the care of your property in the event that you become disabled or die. You also should appoint someone to make your medical decisions in the event that you are too sick to make them yourself. You can do so by signing a Health Care Proxy."

George refused "Why bother with a Health Care Proxy? I probably will never need anyone to assist me. And even if I did, my sons will tell the doctor what I want."

The attorney suggested "If you don't want to appoint a Health Care Agent, then at least let people know what kind of medical treatment you want in the event that you are too ill to speak for yourself. For example, do you want intravenous feeding in the event that you are so ill that there is no hope of recovery?"

"You mean sign a Living Will?"

The attorney explained "The Living Will tells your doctor whether you do, or do not want life-sustaining medical intervention should you be terminally ill with no hope of recovery."

George said he would think about it. But he didn't.

He had other things on his mind. George's wife died the previous year and George was beginning to work through his grief. He recently met Wanda. Although she was considerably younger that George, they found they had much in common.

Their relationship progressed over the next several months, even though his sons made "jokes" about their age difference. They did not have the courage to make jokes or discuss the thing that really was bothering them, namely that Wanda did not work and that George was giving her substantial sums of money. All that seemed to be forgotten, when their father suddenly took ill.

George had a stroke while driving a car. He suffered serious injuries and lapsed into a coma. The prognosis was not encouraging. George's heart was failing and he was having difficulty breathing. The doctors said they could put him on a ventilator, but even using heroic measures, there was little hope that he would survive. And if he did live, the stroke was so damaging that it was doubtful that he could recover enough to have any quality of life.

Wanda pleaded to keep him alive. "Let's try everything. If he doesn't improve we can always discontinue life support systems later."

George's sons did not see it that way. "Why torture him with electric shocks, needles and breathing tubes? Let him pass on peacefully."

George never signed a Living Will so no one knew whether he would have wanted life support systems to be applied. He never signed a Health Care Proxy to appoint someone to make his medical decisions in the event he was unable to do so. In the absence of a Health Care Proxy the doctors had no choice but to consult with his sons. Under New York law, the sons were 3rd in priority. Wanda was 6th.

The Do-Not-Resuscitate Order was signed.

George died.

A Health Care Estate Plan 9

We have discussed an Estate Plan as it relates to the distribution or management of your Estate once you are deceased. But in this age of extended life expectancy, a more important topic is how to manage and preserve your Estate in the event of a debilitating illness. As life expectancy increases, so does the percentage of the population who suffer incapacity from debilitating strokes, Alzheimer's disease or Parkinsons' disease. It is estimated that more than half of the population who are 85 or older, suffer some degree of dementia. Your best Estate Plan could be sabotaged by lengthy or incapacitating illness. In this chapter we will explore ways to pay for the health care that you may require as you age.

In addition to paying for your health care, you need to consider who will care for your finances and every day physical needs in the event that you are too ill to do so yourself. A *Health Care Estate Plan* is a plan designed to care for your person and property in the event of an incapacitating illness. In the last chapter we discussed how you can appoint a Health Care Agent to care for your person in the event of your incapacity. But there is still the problem of who will care for your property. In this chapter we will discuss how you can appoint someone to care for your property and manage your finances in the event of your incapacity.

The optimum way to provide for the care of your property in the event of your incapacity is to set up a Trust appointing a Successor Trustee to care for your property according to the directions given in your Trust. You can be Trustee of the funds while you have capacity. Should you become incapacitated, then the person you name as Successor Trustee will take over. But if you do not have sufficient assets to justify the cost of employing an attorney to draft a Trust, then there are other strategies that you can use to solve the problem.

THE JOINT ACCOUNT

You can set up a joint checking account so that a trusted family member can write checks on the account. Of course there are all the inherent problems of a joint account that we discussed in Chapter 2. You can avoid many of those problems by limiting the amount of money that can be accessed by the family member. For example, you can arrange your finances so that all of your bills are paid from a single checking account and your family member can access that account, only.

THE CONVENIENCE ACCOUNT

If you set up a joint account, your family member will own whatever is in the account should your die. If this is not as you wish, you can instruct the bank that this is a *Convenience Account* and that in the event of your death the family member may no longer access your account. But ultimately the family member must be trustworthy because the bank is under no duty to stop your family member from writing checks on your account until the bank learns of your death (Banking 678).

GUARDIANSHIP: A GOOD THING TO AVOID

The joint or convenience account solves the problem of how to pay your bills in the event you are temporarily ill. It does not solve the problem of how to manage your business affairs in the event of an extended illness. For example, suppose you have a stroke and can no longer be cared for at home. Should it be necessary for you to sell your home and move to an assisted living facility, then no one will have the authority to sell the house for you. In such case, the Court will need to appoint a Guardian to manage your finances, and if you did not appoint a Health Care Agent, to make your health care decisions as well.

Setting up the guardianship is time consuming and expensive. When someone asks the Court to determine whether you are able to manage your person or property, the Court will set a competency hearing. Before conducting the hearing, the Court will appoint a Court Evaluator to visit you and explain your rights under New York law. You can have your own attorney to represent you at the hearing. If you do not have an attorney, the Court can appoint one for you. If it is determined that you are incapacitated, there will be a hearing to decide who will serve as your Guardian. Your attorney will represent you at that hearing as well (Mental Hyg. 81.09, 81.10).

The Court may decide to appoint a Guardian of your person or property, or both. If a Guardian of your property is appointed he will take possession of your assets and file an inventory with the Court. The Court may order your Guardian to obtain a bond for the protection of your assets. Each year the Guardian must account to the Court for monies spent. Your Guardian may need to employ an accountant to help prepare the inventory and annual accounting (Mental Hyg. 81.25, 81.31, 81.32).

If a Guardian of your person is appointed, he will see to your health care. He will need to prepare and file a report each year regarding your well-being. The Guardian will need to employ an attorney to establish and maintain the Guardianship. The Guardian and his attorney are entitled to reasonable compensation for these services (Mental Hyg. 81.28)

Court filing fees, the Court Evaluator's fee, the cost of a bond, accounting fees, the Guardian's fee, your attorney's fee and the Guardian's attorney fees, all are paid from your Estate (that's your money!)

Guardianship procedures are expensive to set up and maintain. Curious that so many people worry about how to avoid Probate, when the greater concern should be how to avoid guardianship. Consider that it is not all that hard to arrange your finances so that no Probate is necessary. The cost to administer your Estate should be $0. Even with a full Probate procedure, whatever it costs to Probate your Estate is a one-time expense. And Probate is a one-time procedure. Once monies are distributed to your beneficiaries, it is over. Not so if you become incapacitated. It can cost thousands of dollars to set up the guardianship; and more money to care for you and your property each year. And this expense goes on, year after year, until you are returned to capacity, or die.

As with Probate it is not all that hard to avoid these unnecessary charges to your Estate. To avoid the need for a Guardian of your person, you can appoint a Health Care Agent to make your medical decisions should you be too ill to do so yourself (see Page 160). To avoid the need for a Guardian of your property, you can set up a Trust and appoint a Successor Trustee to care for your property in the event of your incapacity. For those of limited means, the **Durable Power of Attorney** is the next best Estate plan.

A POWER OF ATTORNEY FOR FINANCES

A Power of Attorney is a legal document by which someone (the **Principal**) gives another (his **Agent** or **Attorney-In-Fact**) authority to do certain acts on behalf of the Principal. If you wish to have someone to be able to conduct business on your behalf in the event of your incapacity, then you can make the Power of Attorney **durable** by including the phrase "This durable power of attorney shall not be affected by my subsequent disability or incompetence."

There is a statutory SHORT FORM OF POWER OF ATTORNEY (General Obligations 5-1501) that you can copy at your local law library or you can download it from the Internet:

NEW YORK STATUTE WEB SITE
http://assembly.state.ny.us./ALIS

You can give your Attorney-In-Fact general powers to manage your finances and do much the same with your property as you can do yourself, such as:
⇨ buy or sell real property on your behalf;
⇨ buy or sell personal property for you;
⇨ trade in securities (stocks, bonds, etc.)
⇨ pay your bills and/or taxes;
⇨ operate your business;
⇨ have access to your safe deposit box;
⇨ borrow money on your behalf;
⇨ purchase insurance policies and name beneficiaries;
⇨ sue or defend a law suit on your behalf;
⇨ apply for government benefits on your behalf;
⇨ have access to your business and personal records.

You can even give your Attorney-In-Fact power to make gifts of your property in accordance with your Estate Plan, for example, you can direct him to give certain family members up to $11,000 in gifts each year.

Notice that there are many things that your Attorney-In-Fact can do for you personally, such as suing or defending a law suit on your behalf or applying for government benefits. Even if you have a Trust, it is important to appoint an Attorney-In-Fact under a Durable Power of Attorney to do these important personal things, in the event you are unable to do so yourself. Your Trust can only authorize your Successor Trustee to manage property that is placed in your Trust. Your Successor Trustee has no authority over you, personally. But you can give him (or anyone else) that authority by making him your Attorney-In-Fact under a Power of Attorney.

GENERAL VS. LIMITED POWER OF ATTORNEY

You can sign a Power of Attorney giving your Attorney-In-Fact broad general powers. With these powers your Attorney-In-Fact can do much the same with your property as you can. If this is of concern to you, instead of giving a General Power of Attorney, you can give a *Limited Power of Attorney* and restrict the things your Attorney-In-Fact can do to just those things authorized in the document.

One power that should be specifically granted in your Power of Attorney, is the power to apply for government benefits, in the event of your incapacity. In the next chapter we will be discussing the many things you can do to qualify for Medicaid eligibility, but if you are suddenly incapacitated, and unable to apply yourself, you need to give someone authority to take the necessary steps to apply for benefits on your behalf.

Even if you do not wish to give someone control over your finances at this time, you should give someone a Limited Power of Attorney with the power to apply for government benefits for you should you be unable to do so yourself.

Limited or General, the operative word in any Power of Attorney is POWER. Once your Attorney-In-Fact has authority to act, he essentially steps in your shoes and can do whatever you gave him authority to do. Your primary consideration in choosing an Attorney-In-Fact is trustworthiness. You need to choose someone who will follow your instructions and put the Power of Attorney to the use you intended. You need to choose someone, who, when using your Power of Attorney, will always put your interests ahead of his.

You may be less concerned with trustworthiness than the loss of independence. But the thing to keep in mind is that you still have the power to do all of the things you gave your Attorney-In-Fact authority to do. The only difference is that now, you both have the power to conduct your business transactions.

Of course, shared authority is still less independent than having sole authority; so you might hesitate to give someone a Power of Attorney until it is needed. The problem with waiting until it is needed is that you may be too sick to sign the document. There are two simple solutions to this dilemma — keeping the document in your possession until needed, or making the document effective only upon your incapacity.

RESTRICTING ACCESS TO THE DOCUMENT

Your Attorney-In-Fact under a Power of Attorney cannot operate on your behalf unless he has possession of the original Power of Attorney and presents it to whoever he wants to rely on that document. For example, if your Attorney-In-Fact wants to use the Power of Attorney to sell one of your securities, he will need to produce the original document and perhaps sign an Affidavit saying that the Power of Attorney is still in effect and that you did not revoke that Power of Attorney.

Before anyone (a bank, stockbroker, closing agent, etc.) will accept the Power of Attorney they will want to see the original document so that they are assured that your Attorney-In-Fact has authority to transact business on your behalf. If you keep the original document in your possession and do not give anyone a copy, your Attorney-In-Fact will not be able to act for you.

The only problem with this arrangement is that you need to arrange to make the document accessible to your Attorney-In-Fact in the event of your incapacity. If your Attorney-In-Fact is a trusted family member, then you can tell your Attorney-In-Fact where your Durable Power of Attorney is located and how to get possession of the document should the need arise.

MAKE IT EFFECTIVE ONLY UPON YOUR INCAPACITY

A better solution may be to sign a "springing" Durable Power of Attorney that is not operational until your family doctor and/or independent physician say that you are incapacitated and unable to manage your finances.

Your Attorney-In-Fact can hold the original document, but cannot use it until it "springs to life" when a doctor determines that you are too ill to care for your property.

There is a statutory form of this type of Power of Attorney that you can copy from your local Law Library or download from the New York Statute Web site.

It is General Obligations Law 5-1506 and is entitled:
DURABLE GENERAL POWER OF ATTORNEY
EFFECTIVE AT A FUTURE TIME.

It is relatively simple and inexpensive to head off guardianship. All you need do is appoint an Attorney-In-Fact under a Durable Power of Attorney to manage your finances, and a Health Care Agent under a Health Care Proxy to make your medical care decisions. These documents authorize people of your choice to care for you and your property in the event of your incapacity. But, despite your best plans, something unusual could happen causing a Court to decide that you need a Guardian. For example, suppose you disappear and cannot be found after a diligent search. It might be necessary to have a Court appoint a Guardian to manage your property in your absence. Or perhaps you develop an addiction or a mental illness causing self-destructive behavior. Your friends or family might decide that you are in need of protection and ask a Court to appoint a Guardian to care for you.

Although it may not be possible to avoid all guardianship procedures, you can have a measure of control over your fate. New York statute gives you the right to name the person of your choice to serve as your Guardian (Mental Hyg. 81.17). You can do this by including a provision in your Health Care Proxy that you nominate your Health Care Agent to serve as guardian of your person, should the need arise. You can include a similar provision in your Durable Power of Attorney, i.e., that your Attorney-In-Fact is to serve as the Guardian of your property.

The Judge will honor your wishes and appoint your choice of Guardian unless the Court finds he is not qualified to serve for some reason, such as being a convicted felon (Surrogates 707).

PROVIDING FOR LONG TERM CARE

The good news is: You are going to live longer.
The bad news is: It's going to cost you.

Scientists are doing a great job of prolonging life, but unless they find Ponce De Leon's fountain, the general population will age. Along with age comes infirmities. Eyes fail. Hearing diminishes. Mobility declines. Digestive systems either speed up or slow down, all to the discomfort of the unhappy occupant of the body. It's all part of the "golden" years.

The pharmacology industry is well motivated to produce drugs that manage the ills associated with aging. Their research has led to a wealth of pharmaceutic products that do not cure, but do allow people to live relatively comfortably into advanced age. The only problem is the cost of these drugs. Medicare covers the treatment of life-threatening brushes with heart disease, stroke, cancer and diabetes; but, as of this writing, Medicare does not pay for maintenance medication that is often necessary once the condition is stabilized.

Medicare is also limited in long term care coverage. It does not pay for extended nursing care. Medicare pays for the first 20 days of skilled nursing care. Medicare pays the excess over $101.50** for days 21 through 100. That means you pay $8,120 for the next 80 days. After 100 days, you are on your own. A nursing home stay of one or two years can wipe out the life savings of most working people. Once savings are gone, the government provides care in the form of Medicaid coverage.

**This is the value as we went to print. The federal government adjusts the amount each year.

If you have no assets to speak of, and an income beneath the poverty level, then long-term nursing care is the least of your worries. Medicaid will cover the cost of your medical and nursing care needs. And no need to worry if you are wealthy. You have more than enough money to pay for any care that you might need. The rest of us need to think about ways to provide for long-term health care.

For those concerned about the loss of life savings because of illness, there is supplemental and/or long-term care insurance. There are many different insurance plans available. You can call the National Association of Insurance Commissioners at (816) 842-3600 and they will forward to you, free of charge, the publication:

A SHOPPER'S GUIDE TO LONG TERM CARE INSURANCE

The New York State Agency on Aging offers insurance counseling. If you have a specific question, you can call the Senior Citizen Hotline at (800) 342-9871. Out of state call (518) 474-4425.

You can also get information by visiting the Office of Aging Web site.

 NEW YORK STATE OFFICE FOR THE AGING
http://www.aging.state.ny.us

THE PROBLEM OF COST AND ELIGIBILITY

Long term care insurance sounds like the perfect solution, until you start examining the cost. The cost isn't too bad if you are comparatively young, say in your 50s. But can you imagine paying that premium each month until you are in your 80s and never needing nursing care?

Many decide to wait till they are old and going downhill. But that just brings other problems. The older you are, the greater the cost of insurance. And there is the risk that you will be refused coverage because of a "pre-existing" condition, i.e., the insurance company may consider you to be too great a risk for them to insure.

Some insurance companies have come up with an insurance plan that may offer a solution. They offer a long term care insurance for those in good health. If you purchase the policy and never need long term care, then the policy converts to a life insurance policy upon your death. When you are shopping around, consider including a combination long-term care insurance and life insurance policy in your investigation.

The Long Term Care Security Act (Public Law 106-265) was passed by Congress to take effect in October, 2002. The law is designed to make long term care insurance available to federal and postal employees, members of the uniformed services, civilian and military retirees, and their qualified relatives.

You can call the Office of Personnel Management at (800) 582-3337 for information about the program or visit their Web site.

 OFFICE OF PERSONNEL MANAGEMENT
http://www.opm.gov/insure/ltc

The National Association Of Retired Federal Employees ("NARFE") has been actively involved in developing this legislation. You can get updates on the law by calling their legislative hotline in Alexandria, Virginia at (703) 838-7780, or by visiting their Web site.

 NARFE WEB SITE
http://www.narfe.org

For some people long term care insurance is not an option. An elderly person living on a low fixed income may not have enough money to pay the monthly premium for a long term care insurance policy. And long term care insurance is not an option for the person who has been diagnosed with a chronic, debilitating disease.

People in such a position worry that they may need to deplete their life savings, just to pay for a year or two of nursing care.

Both of these problems can be solved by using current law to become qualified for Medicaid. Medicaid is a public assistance program that is funded jointly by the federal and state government. There are state and federal laws governing who may become eligible for the program.

A *Medicaid Qualifying Plan* is a plan that takes both state and federal laws into consideration. Operating within the boundaries of these laws, those who are concerned about becoming impoverished in order to pay for long-term care, seek to preserve and protect their Estate by implementing a Medicaid Qualifying Plan.

There has been controversy about plans that are designed to qualify a person for Medicaid. Some think that to intentionally arrange finances to qualify for Medicaid is immoral — a legal method of working the system.

Those people may argue: "Why are such things allowed? After all, wasn't Medicaid designed to help poor people? Why should people be allowed to make themselves poor to get on the public dole??

Those who feel they need to qualify for Medicaid have a different point of view. They may argue:

"I worked all my life and hoped to leave a few pennies for the kids. Why did I work so hard? To give it all to a nursing home? I paid my taxes just like everyone else. The government pays hundreds of thousands of dollars for people on Medicare to have open heart surgery, and they pay for lengthy and expensive cancer treatments. Why should those who have Alzheimer's or Parkinsons or those who suffer a debilitating stroke, not be entitled to receive similar benefits?"

Although we can understand and appreciate both points of view, our job, as we see it, is to just explain the law as it exists when we went to print. We feel that it is important to do so because many people take a position (pro or con) based on what they perceive the law to be, and not based upon the law as it actually is.

We hope that once the reader understands what it takes to qualify for Medicaid in the state of New York, he can decide for himself whether the law is basically fair to the people who need to qualify, or whether it is flawed (either too restrictive or too liberal) and needs to be changed.

Hopefully, those with a strong opinion will share those views with their legislators.

A Medicaid Qualifying Plan 10

A better name for this chapter might be "A Health Care Contingency Plan." A lengthy stay in a nursing home is something most of us do not want to even think about, much less prepare for. Why prepare for something that may never happen? Yet as we age, there is that nagging "what if?" "What if I need long term nursing care? How will I pay for it?"

An effective way to put this anxiety at rest is to have a contingency plan. To form a contingency plan, you need to know your options. In this case, your options are directly related to your ability to pay for that care. But it is hard to predict future fortunes. People win the lottery. Those with a large portfolio may have their fortunes disappear in a market melt-down. There is no need for concern if it turns out that you can afford to pay for your own nursing care; and there is no concern should you become impoverished because the government will provide care for you. The worst case scenario is that you will be able to afford long-term care, but at the cost of your life savings.

In this chapter we will discuss options available to you under that worst case scenario. We will explain current state and federal law as it relates to qualifying for Medicaid programs.

Once you know the law, you will be able to form a contingency health care plan that is right for you.

WHO IS ENTITLED TO MEDICAID?

Medicaid is a program that provides medical and long term nursing care for people with low income and limited resources. The program is funded and regulated by both federal and state government. The governing agency for the federal government is the Centers for Medicare and Medicaid Services (formerly the Health Care Financing Administration). In New York, the program is administered by the Department of Social Services.

Medicaid is an entitlement program, meaning that whoever qualifies for the program is entitled to receive benefits under that program, and conversely those who do not qualify are not entitled to any Medicaid benefits.

There are many benefits offered under Medicaid, from health care for mothers and children; to community based services for those who need some assistance with their health care; to full nursing care for those who need assistance with dressing, bathing, feeding, walking and toileting. We will limit our discussion of Medicaid to those who qualify medically and who need full nursing care. You can get information about other programs by calling the New York State Department of Social Services of Health at (518) 474-8216. New York City residents can call the Human Resources Administration Medical Assistance Program at (718) 291-1900. Residents of the five boroughs can call toll free at (877) 472-8411.

You can also get information about Medicaid from the New York State Department of Health Web site.

 NEW YORK STATE DEPARTMENT OF HEALTH
http://www.health.state.ny.us

When a person applies for Medicaid (the "Applicant"**) the Department of Social Services ("DSS") will investigate his medical condition, income, and resources (i.e., assets). Persons who are receiving Supplemental Security Income ("SSI") may be automatically eligible for Medicaid because the requirements for these programs are much the same. If a person is not receiving SSI, he may be eligible for Medicaid if he is 65 or older, or blind, or disabled (Social Services Law 366(1), 366 (2), 366 (3)).

NO LIMIT ON INCOME

In New York there is no limit on the amount of income earned by the Applicant each month, because once he is approved and becomes a Recipient of Medicaid benefits whatever he earns will be sent to the nursing home to pay for his care. Of course should the Applicant have a very high income, there would be no reason to apply for Medicaid because he could afford to pay for his own nursing home care.

The Recipient is allowed to keep a certain amount of his income each month (currently $50) for his personal needs, such as clothing or hair cuts. The rest of his income will go to the nursing home. The amount contributed by the Recipient is supplemented by Medicaid program.

Although there is no limit on the Applicant's income, there is a limit for his assets (currently $3,800). An Applicant who is over the resource limit on the day he applies for Medicaid needs to "spend down" his assets to $3,800. He will be eligible for Medicaid on the first day of the month in which his assets are $3,800 or less (18 New York Code, Rules & Regulations (NYCRR) 360-4.1(b).

** For simplicity, we will use the male gender for the Applicant and the female gender for his spouse.

If the Applicant is married, there are limits to his spouse's assets as well. If his spouse resides at home in the community (i.e., not in a nursing home) she is referred to as the **Community Spouse**. Prior to 1988, the Community Spouse was expected to use whatever assets she had to pay for the nursing care of her spouse. The Applicant could not qualify for Medicaid until they both were virtually impoverished. In addition to being unfair to the Community Spouse, this was not good government policy because it often resulted in the impoverished spouse turning to local government social service systems for support.

The Medicaid provisions of the Medicare Catastrophic Act of 1988 remedied the situation by considering the income and assets of the couple as being part of a common pot and allowing the Community Spouse to keep a portion of their combined income and assets. As of the date we went to print, the federal government allows the Community Spouse to keep up to $2,232 of their combined monthly income for her support. She is also allowed to keep up to $89,280 of their combined *resources*, i.e. assets that are countable for the purpose of qualifying for Medicaid (42 U.S.C. 1382b). These values are adjusted for cost of living increases.

Notice that these are maximum values set by the federal government. States have the right to administer the Medicaid program according to their state law, provided their state law is within federal guidelines. This being the case, the actual amount received by the Community spouse varies significantly state to state.

In New York, the least amount allowed for the support of the Community spouse is $2,232 per month. This value is called the **Minimum Monthly Maintenance Needs Allowance**.

THE SPOUSE'S INCOME

The Department of Social Services allows the Community Spouse to keep up to $2,232 from the couple's common pot of income. If for some reason (high medical bills, the need for special care, etc.) the Community Spouse needs more than $2,232 a month, she can appeal to have that value increased. See the end of this chapter for a discussion of the appeal process.

If the Community Spouse has a monthly income that is greater than $2,232, the DSS may require the spouse to contribute the 25% of that excess to pay for the nursing home (18 NYCRR 360-4.10(b)(5)).

Some examples might better explain these rules.
Suppose the Community Spouse has an income of $2,000, and the DSS determines that she needs the full $2,232 for her monthly maintenance. DSS will allow $232 of the Recipient's income to go to his Community Spouse. Suppose instead that the Community Spouse has a fixed income of $3,000. In that case, the Community Spouse will need to contribute 25% of any amount of her income that exceeds $2,232: $3,000 - $2,232 = $768
Spousal contribution: .25 X $768 = $192

Each month the Community Spouse will need to contribute $192 toward the nursing care of the Medicaid recipient. Should the income of the Community Spouse increase or decease then the amount contributed is adjusted accordingly.

Assets owned by the Applicant or his spouse, are considered to be available to the Applicant for purposes of Medicaid eligibility. Under federal law, the Community Spouse is entitled to keep a share of the couple assets up to the current maximum of $89,280. That share is called the **Community Spouse Resource Allowance** (42 U.S.C. 1396r-5(c)(2), 1396r-5f).

In New York, the Community Spouse to allowed to keep half of their common pot of assets with a minimum value of $74,820 up to the federal maximum value of $89,280. For example, suppose the couple own $77,000 between them. The Community Spouse is entitled to a minimum amount of $74,820. The Applicant is allowed to keep the remaining $2,180. All other things being equal, the Applicant should qualify for Medicaid.

But suppose the couple have $150,000 between them. In that case, the Community spouse's Resource Allowance is half of their common pot of assets, namely $75,000. The Applicant may not have more than $3,800. He is free to transfer anything over that value to his spouse; but that still leaves them with an excess of $71,200.

$$\$75,000 + \$3,800 = \$78,800$$
$$\$150,000 - \$78,800 = \$71,200$$

The first question to ask in such a situation is whether all of their assets count as a resource.

WHAT COUNTS AS A RESOURCE?

All real or personal property, owned by the Applicant, or his spouse, that can be converted to cash and used for their support is a resource. This includes their bank accounts, certificates of deposit, stocks and bonds, etc. There are assets that can be converted to cash, but do not count as a resource. These items are called "Excluded Assets" or "Non- Countable Resources" or "Disregards." We will refer to them as *Exempt Resources.* The following items are Exempt Resources and are not counted as a resource for purposes of Medicaid Eligibility.

EXEMPT RESOURCES

ESSENTIAL PERSONAL PROPERTY

Personal property being used by the Applicant or his spouse are exempt items. They include:

⇨ wedding and engagement rings, regardless of their value;

⇨ home furnishings and appliances, books, household tools

⇨ tools and equipment which are necessary for a trade, occupation or business.

The Department of Social Services will consider heirlooms, coin or stamp collections as essential personal property, provided they are not worth very much. Household items that are worth a significant amount of money, such as a valuable antique or an expensive painting, can be counted by DSS as a resource.

LIFE INSURANCE

⇨ An insurance policy owned by the Applicant is exempt if the face value (the amount paid at death) is $1,500 or less. If the Applicant owns more than one policy on the same person, then they are exempt, provided the sum of their face values is not greater than $1,500.

If the face value of the policy is more than $1,500, then the Cash Surrender Value of the policy is counted as a resource. You can contact the insurance company to obtain the current Cash Surrender Value.

BURIAL ARRANGEMENTS

⇨ Burial spaces for the Applicant or his family (spouse, child, parent, sibling and the spouse of a family member) are Exempt Resources. This includes prepaid burial space items such as grave sites, mausoleums, urns, niches, etc. Opening and closing the grave, headstones, and headstone engravings are also considered burial space items.

⇨ An Irrevocable Preneed Funeral Agreement as described in Chapter 8 is an Exempt Resource.

⇨ A burial fund of up to $1,500 is exempt, provided the fund is in a separate account and clearly identified as a burial account. The burial fund is not available if there is an Irrevocable Preneed Funeral Agreement of $1,500 or more, or if there is an life insurance policy of $1,500.

If the Applicant has a revocable Preneed Funeral Agreement, the Department of Social Services will allow him to make that plan irrevocable so that it will qualify as an Exempt Resource. They will not allow the Community Spouse to do so, however they will allow the Community Spouse to set up her own burial fund of up to $1,500.

AUTOMOBILE

⇨   One car that is allowed as an Exempt Resource regardless of its value.

THE HOME

⇨   The primary residence (home, condominium, cooperative apartment, or mobile home) that is occupied by the Applicant or his family (spouse, minor or dependent child, dependent relative) is an Exempt Asset.

The Applicant's home is an Exempt Resource so long as it is his primary residence or that of his spouse or minor child. If the Applicant is in a nursing home, and no spouse or family member lives in the home, it remains an Exempt Resource, provided the Applicant has indicated that he intends to return home.

RETIREMENT FUNDS

⇨   The cash value of a retirement fund (pension plan, IRA, Keogh plans, etc.) is an Exempt Resource, provided the Applicant, or his spouse, is receiving periodic payments; i.e., is on a "permanent pay" status.

If the Applicant (or his spouse) is not entitled to periodic payments, but can withdraw monies from the account, then the retirement fund counts as a resource. If there is a penalty for the early withdrawal of the retirement fund, then the value of the resource is the amount that is available after paying the penalty.

BUSINESS PROPERTY

⇨   Property used in the ordinary course of an ongoing business in which the Applicant or his spouse have an ownership interest is an Exempt Resource. This includes inventories, supplies, tools, equipment, livestock, machinery, motor vehicles, etc.

The building that houses the business; i.e., a factory or store is also exempt, provided it is an asset of the business. Other income producing property, such as an apartment building is not considered to be an Exempt Resource. The equity value (market value less mortgage balance) of the apartment building is counted as a resource.

JOINTLY OWNED BANK ACCOUNT

DSS considers the full value of a jointly owned bank account to be available to the Applicant, or his spouse; unless another joint owner contributed to the account. For example, if the Applicant owns a joint bank account with his son, the entire balance counts as a resource unless it can be shown that the son contributed his own money to that account. The monies contributed by the son do not count as a resource.

OTHER EXEMPT ASSETS

We have listed many of the more common items that the Department of Social Services considers to be Exempt Assets. But this is not a complete list. There are other items that DSS will not include as part of the Applicant's resources. You can find the complete list, including all of the legal references that allow the asset to be excluded, at the Department of Health Web site. You can find the information by looking up "Information For Research" and then "Medicaid."

 NEW YORK STATE DEPARTMENT OF HEALTH
http://www.health.state.ny.us

Now that we know what does (and does not) count as a resource, the next question is what options are available to an Applicant who has too many assets.

THE SPEND DOWN OPTION

Suppose our couple have $150,000 between them. If the Applicant tries to qualify for Medicaid at that point, the New York Department of Social Services will explain that it is his spouse's duty to pay for Applicant's nursing care with their excess resources of $71,200.

Those with no knowledge of the law, might think the only option available to this couple is to pay for his nursing care until the $71,200 runs out. Those who read the previous pages, might suggest that the couple check to see whether they can use the money to purchase items that do not count as a resource. For example, they can make funeral or burial arrangements, if they have not already done so. The Community Spouse may decide to buy household items such as furniture, a television set, a stove or refrigerator, etc.

This Spend-down Option is permissible because both state and federal law give the Applicant and his spouse the right to own an Exempt Resource.

REPAIRING EXEMPT ITEMS

Paying money to repair exempt items is a good spend-down strategy. Perhaps the exempt family car needs new brakes, or tires. The Community Spouse may decide to replace the car with a new model.

If the house is in need of repair or improvement, then this is the time to fix it up. A new heating, plumbing or electrical system can use up funds quickly. If the couple do not own their own home, the Community Spouse might consider using the excess cash as a down-payment on a home.

SPEND-DOWN BY PAYING DEBTS

Some sceptics might think $71,200 is a lot of money to spend down. Maybe the couple previously made their funeral and burial arrangements. Perhaps they really don't need (or want) new furniture or appliances. In such case, the solution may be to pay off all of their outstanding debts. The couple can reduce their credit card balance to $0. If they owe money on the exempt family car, they can pay off that loan. Excess resources can be used to pay down the mortgage on the couple's home.

Paying off loans is a valid spend-down strategy because it is just a return of monies given to the Applicant by the lender for the purchase of an Exempt Resource (car, house, clothing, household items). But the Applicant or his Community Spouse will need to prove to the DSS, that the monies he spent were used to pay off a valid debt.

If a credit card debt was paid, DSS will want to see the original contract with the company and the monthly bill showing what items were purchased. If the Applicant repaid a car loan, DSS will want to see the original promissory note (marked "PAID"), as well as other loan items, such as a chattel mortgage. If the money was used to pay down a mortgage on their home, DSS will want to see the original loan documents as well as documents showing the new balance, or a satisfaction of mortgage, if it was paid in full.

Suppose the couple with the excess assets has little income. For example, suppose it is determined that the Community Spouse needs at least $2,232 per month, but the couple's combined income is only $1,500. In such case, she can ask the DSS to allow her to keep as much of their excess assets as is necessary to give her this minimum income. In effect, she needs to ask DSS "May I keep more than my Resource Allowance so that the income from this property will help to get me to that minimum income?"

But she could also take another tack, and simply refuse to spend-down her resources. She could say "I won't spend down. It will cause me undue hardship to do so." This is called the "Just say no" strategy. In legal terms it is called **Spousal Refusal.** In such circumstances, the Federal law allows the Applicant to receive Medicaid benefits even though the Community Spouse's resources exceed the Resource Allowance. In fact, under Federal law, the Community Spouse can refuse to spend-down even though her income might be greater than $2,232; provided the state has the right to proceed against the spouse (i.e., sue the Community Spouse) (42 U.S.C. 1396r-5(c)(3)). Under New York law, the state has that right (Social Services Law 366).

That being the case, a New York Applicant cannot be denied Medicaid if his Community Spouse refuses to use her own resources, or even their joint resources to pay for the nursing care of the Applicant. The Community Spouse can tell the Department of Social Services that she needs that money for herself, and that she will not contribute anything to his care.

The reader must think this very strange. "You mean the spouse can "just say no" and the Department of Social Services will say "O.K.?"

The answer to that question is "yes."

When you think about it, the law makes sense. Why should a very sick Applicant be denied nursing care just because his spouse refuses to cooperate? Better to take care of the ill spouse and sue the Community Spouse later.

The reader might wonder "Why would anyone go this route? Why would anyone risk being sued? And if they are sued, no doubt they will lose."

The answer is that in some cases, Spousal Refusal makes economic sense. The Department of Social Services sets the amount the state will pay monthly to the nursing home for the care of Medicaid patients. That amount is less than the amount charged by the nursing home for private paying patients, even though federal law requires that the Medicaid patient receive the same level of care as a private paying patient (42 U.S.C. 1396r(c)4).

The amount the Department of Social Services contributes is reduced by the amount contributed from the Applicant's income. For example, suppose the nursing facility charges $7,000 per month for a private patient and $6,000 for a Medicaid patient. If the Applicant's income is $2,050 a month, he keeps $50 for his personal needs. The remaining $2,000 is paid to the nursing home. The Department pays $4,000 per month.

As explained on page 185, all that may be required of the Community Spouse is to contribute 25% of her income in excess of the Minimum Monthly Maintenance Needs Allowance, towards that $4,000 per month. If the Department of Social Services sues under current law, it will be to recover that 25% of the excess income.

That's quite an economic incentive. Specifically, if in the given example, the Community Spouse uses her excess resources , it will cost $7,000 a month to pay for her spouse's care as a private patient. By refusing, her husband gets the same care as a private paying patient. His income is contributed towards his care, but the Community Spouse keeps her own income and resources, and the income generated by her resources each month.

On the other end of the economic scale is the cost of attorney fees to defend the action. More important, is the stress of the unknown. Both state and federal laws can quickly change. Instead of suing for just the 25% of the excess income, they might sue the Community Spouse for every penny spent by the government for his care. In the given example, that would be $4,000 per month. They could even pass a law saying that if the Community Spouse loses the case, she could be liable for Court costs and the Department of Social Services' attorney fees.

Many Community Spouses are themselves aged and not in the of best health. Not knowing when or if the state will assert its right to have the Community Spouse contribute funds, may be too stressful.

There are other strategies discussed in this Chapter, that might work as well, without the fear of being sued.

A spend-down strategy that is currently allowed by both federal and state law is the of purchase of *Immediate Pay Annuity*; i.e., an annuity whose payments begin the month after the purchase and continue for a fixed period of time. For purposes of Medicaid eligibility, that fixed period of time is based on the life expectancy of the annuitant (in this case, the Community Spouse).

The life expectancy of the annuitant is determined by referring to the actuarial table as published by the Centers for Medicare and Medicaid Services; State Medicaid Manual, Part 3 (SM3 3259.1) "Life Expectancy Tables— Males and Life Expectancy Tables—Females."

You can find excerpts from that table, at the author's Web site.

 VINCENT J. RUSSO & ASSOCIATES, P. C.
http://www.russoelderlaw.com

UNASSIGNABLE AND IRREVOCABLE
The annuity contract cannot be transferred, sold or assigned. It must be irrevocable. In other words, nothing can be changed; not the monthly payment, nor the number of payments, nor the identity of the Annuitant.

NO CASH VALUE
The annuity contract must have no value other than the monthly payments to the annuitant.

ACTUARIALLY SOUND

The annuity contract must be ***actuarially sound,*** meaning that the schedule of monthly payments does not extend beyond the annuitant's life expectancy and that the money invested in the annuity is returned to the annuitant at a "reasonable" rate of return. The Department of Social Services determines what is a reasonable rate based on current market conditions. Companies in the business of selling such annuities generally offer the annuity at a rate that is acceptable to DSS.

If you are purchasing an annuity to qualify for Medicaid, it is important to have your Elder Law attorney, or the agent who is selling the annuity, to verify that the policy meets the DSS criteria for being actuarially sound.

We will refer to an annuity that meets all of these criteria as a ***Medicaid Annuity***.

Purchasing a Medicaid Annuity could solve the problem for the Community Spouse whose has too little income and too much in resources. The Community Spouse can use her excess resources to buy the annuity. She will keep the income from that investment, just as she would if she had the money invested in a stock, bond or Certificate of Deposit. The only difference is that each month part of the principal is return to her as part of that monthly income.

This spend-down strategy can be used by the Community Spouse even when her income is not a problem. But it may not make economic sense if the sum of her monthly income, including the income from the annuity, exceeds $2,232. For example, suppose her only income is $1,000 from Social Security. The Department will allow her to keep $1,232 of her husband's income. If the annuity pays $1,232, she may keep none of her husband's income. All of his income will be used for his nursing care.

If her income plus that of the annuity, puts her over $2,232, then this strategy makes even less economic sense; because in addition to not keeping any of her husband's income, she must contribute 25% of her excess income to his nursing care.

In other words, purchasing the Medicaid Annuity may enable the Applicant to qualify for Medicaid, but it may not result in extra income for Community Spouse. And there are other things to consider:

LOSS OF LIQUIDITY
The Medicaid Annuity is irrevocable. Should her husband die shortly after she purchases the annuity, she cannot cash it in.

FIXED RETURN ON INVESTMENT
Annuities offer a fixed rate of return and there is no way to adjust that rate for periods of inflation. The rate of return on the annuity is set at the time of purchase. We are currently in a period of low inflation. Should there be a period of high inflation, the annuity will still yield the same rate of return as when purchased.

RISK OF LOSS

By purchasing an annuity, the annuitant is giving his money to a company in exchange for the company's promise to pay interest and return part of the principal each month. The company promises to make these payments every month for a certain number of years (the annuitant's life expectancy). Should the company become bankrupt during that period of time, the monies invested may be in jeopardy.

Needless to say, all these concerns need to be addressed before investing in a Medicaid Annuity. Consultation with an Elder Law attorney prior to the purchase is a must.

Although purchasing a Medicaid Annuity may work for the Community Spouse with a low fixed income, it may not be the best strategy for the single Applicant, because any income he receives from the annuity will be used for his nursing care. For example, suppose an unmarried, Applicant who has $100,000 takes suddenly ill, and needs extensive nursing care. Under current law he can purchase keep $3,800 for himself and purchase a Medicaid Annuity for $96,200. If the Applicant is 80 years old, then according to current actuarial tables he has a year life expectancy of 6.98 years. He can name his child as successor annuitant in the event that he does not live out the full term of the policy.

Once he makes the purchase, he can immediately apply for Medicaid. He will of course report the purchase to the DSS. They will examine the terms of the annuity to be sure they satisfy current regulations. If they do and he meets all other requirements, he should qualify for Medicaid.

He's happy because he did not need to spend down his $96,200 in nursing home bills. He's hoping that his condition improves enough so that he can return home. In such case, his nursing care will be paid by Medicaid, and he will continues to receive the income from the annuity when he returns home.

DSS is happy because any income he receives while in the facility will go toward payment of his nursing home bill; leaving that much less for the state to contribute to his care.

His child may or may not be happy depending on whether he believes his father may live longer than expected.

By purchasing the immediate annuity, his father is betting that he will not need nursing care for the next 6.98 years; or if so, then he will not live out the full 6.98 years. If he loses his bet, none of his assets are protected. All of his money will be used to pay for his nursing care. In such case it may be better for him to use a strategy better designed for the single Applicant.

Spend down may not be the best strategy for the single Applicant who is over the asset limit by a significant amount, say $90,000. Sure he can make funeral and burial arrangements; but that will only use up a small portion of his assets. He could buy a car or an expensive television set, but what good are these items to him if he has a progressive disease and it is not expected that he will ever leave the nursing home?

Some may wonder "Why not go into the facility as a paying patient? That will use up his assets pretty quick."

And so it would. But the applicant may have wanted his children to inherit that $90,000. An applicant in such a position may decide to make an *uncompensated transfer* to his children; i.e. he gets nothing in return for the transfer (love and affection don't count).

Should the Applicant make a gift of his funds, the Department of Social Services will impose a *penalty period*, i.e., a period of time that the applicant is disqualified from receiving Medicaid benefits.

The penalty period is computed by dividing the amount transferred by the average monthly cost of nursing home care in the county as determined by the Department of Social Services. The average cost, at the time we went to print, ranges from $5,393 to $8,272, depending on the county. If the Applicant in the above example, decided to transfer $90,000, and the average cost of nursing care in his county is set at $6,000, then he would be disqualified for 15 months, beginning with the month following the month in which the gift was made.

$$90,000/\$6,000 = 15 \text{ months}$$

THE RULE OF HALVES

The strategy of transferring all his assets and waiting a year or two may not be an option if our single Applicant needs immediate nursing care. In such case, the adage "half a loaf is better than none" applies; only in legal circles we refer to it as the **Rule of Halves**.

The concept is simple. The Applicant gives away a certain amount of money to trigger a penalty period for a certain amount of time — yet keeping enough money for his living expenses during the penalty period. For example, suppose our single Applicant who has $90,000 finds that he needs $6,000 month (in addition to his ordinary income) to pay for his nursing care and living expenses. If the average cost of nursing care as set by the DSS in his county is $6,000 and the Applicant gives half of his assets to his child it will trigger a 7 month penalty period.

$$\$45,000/\$6,000 = 7.5 \text{ months.}$$

The fractional part of the penalty period is counted as a resource to the Applicant; specifically, the Department of Social Services will multiply the fraction by the average cost of nursing care and count that value as a resource. In the given example .5 X $6,000 = $3,000.

During that penalty period the Applicant will use the remaining $45,000 to pay for his nursing care. At the end of the 7 months he can apply for Medicaid, provided he has no more than $3,800, including the fractional part of the penalty period.

The Applicant will report the $45,000 transfer to the Department of Social Services, and they will note that the penalty period has passed. All other things equal, the Applicant should qualify for Medicaid at that time.

Of course, this is just a hypothetical case. An Applicant may need more or less than $6,000 to supplement his income each month. The amount he gives away needs to be adjusted accordingly.

Although the Rule of Halves is easy to understand, implementing it needs careful consideration. It is important to consult with an Elder Law attorney who can calculate the proper balance between gift and monies that need to be reserved for the Applicant's care during the penalty period.

JUST GIVE IT ALL AWAY

The strategy we have been discussing can be used if the Applicant needs immediate nursing care. But it may happen that a person is diagnosed with a debilitating, progressive disease, that may ultimately result in a lengthy stay in a nursing facility. A person in such a situation may decide to give his property away, with the hope that he will not need long term nursing care for at least three years.

The three years is the ***look-back period*** that the Department of Social Services uses to investigate the finances of a person who applies for Medicaid. The look-back period starts on the first day of the month in which the Applicant applies for Medicaid and goes back three years from that date. The look-back period increases to five years if there was a transfer into a Trust (42 U.S.C. 1396p(c). If the Department of Social Services determines that the Applicant, or his spouse, made transfers during the look-back period, the DSS will impose a penalty period equal to the sum total of all uncompensated transfers divided by the average cost of nursing care. This is the general rule. It gets more complicated if more than one uncompensated transfer was made during that period.

 THERE IS NO LIMIT ON THE PENALTY PERIOD

Although DSS will only look back 3 years for transfers, there is no limit on the penalty period imposed for that transfer. For example, suppose the Applicant gives his child $300,000. If he applies for Medicaid within three years from the date of transfer, he can be denied Medicaid benefits for more than four years.

$$\$300,000 / \$6,000 = 50 \text{ months } (4.17 \text{ years})$$

Of course the way to avoid the problem is to transfer the funds and not apply any sooner than three full years from the date of the transfer. But if the transfer was made into an irrevocable Trust, the applicant is stuck with the full 50 months; because, as discussed, the state has the right to look back five years if funds were transferred into a Trust.

And incidentally, this is not a game of "Catch me if you can." Under both state and federal law, the Applicant and his spouse (or whoever applies for him) are required to make a full disclosure of transfers made during these periods. Fraudulently obtaining medical assistance through Medicaid is a crime subject to prosecution (Social Services Law 145).

In addition, the Department of Social Services can discontinue all further medical assistance and sue for the cost of Medicaid benefits that were improperly paid (Social Services Law 104).

The reader may be thinking "Yes, but if I don't make a transfer into a Trust, all the law requires is that I report transfers made within the previous 3 years. If I come down with an illness that I know will cause me to deteriorate over a period of time, all I need do is give all my money to my child; be sure to wait three years and I will qualify for Medicaid. My child will keep my money safe. Should I need that money, my child will return as much as I need to me. Money that I don't use will be protected for my child."

The Medicaid Qualifying Plan of giving away all assets and then waiting three years is certainly allowed under the law, but this is a "brute force" approach to the problem. There's no finesse. It is a drastic step to take and fraught with perils. Once the money is transferred, a completed gift is made. The child becomes the legal owner of the money and with all of the obvious "what ifs."

What if the child is sued. Will a Court order the child to use the money you gave to pay the judgment?

What if the child is divorced. Will the Court decide that your child's spouse is entitled to half of that money?

But the real problem is the loss of independence. Being impoverished at a time in your life when you are unable to supplement your income, and when your physical health is declining, can lead to much sadness. Imagine going to your child and asking for money.

Imagine the child thinking, or worse yet, asking
"What's the money for?"

And what if you give the money away and never need nursing care? Medical technology is advancing with amazing speed. Although few cures have been found for mankind's ills, there have been many breakthroughs in their treatment. With modern drugs, many patients are now able to function without the need for long-term care. Even those who have been diagnosed with a progressive disease may not need nursing care for several years — maybe never.

Meanwhile, the money, and your independence, is gone.

Giving all ones money away and then waiting three years works, but at the cost of your independence. Putting money into an irrevocable Trust and waiting 5 years has its risks. A lot can happen in 5 years. You could require full nursing care the day after you transfer your assets into the Trust. Maybe the 5 year look-back is changed to a 6 year look back period.

For those in good health, an alternative is to do nothing until you actually need nursing home care and then implement a Medicaid qualifying strategy at that time. This is not to lull the reader into a false sense of security. Federal and state laws constantly change. Whatever strategy you choose may not be around when you need it. For example, there are those who oppose the use of the Medicaid Annuity. Legislation has been proposed in several states that would restrict its use.

The reason we wrote this chapter was to not to give the reader a definitive Medicaid Qualifying strategy, but rather to give the reader an understanding of the law as it relates to qualifying for Medicaid; and to let the reader know that there are options available should the need arise. And, incidentally, we touched only on the basics***. There are other, more sophisticated, Medicaid Qualifying options available that an experienced Elder Law attorney can explain to you. The prudent thing to do is to visit an Elder Law attorney if and when you become concerned about long term care problem. He can explain current law to you as it relates to qualifying for Medicaid. He can suggest the best path for you to follow, given your set of circumstances.

*** For a more advanced discussion, see NEW YORK ELDER LAW PRACTICE (West Group) by Vincent J. Russo and Marvin Rachlin.

PROTECTING THE HOMESTEAD

We discussed the problem of having cash assets in excess of that allowed under current federal and state law; but what about the person whose only asset of value is his home? As explained earlier in the Chapter, whether the home counts as a Resource for purposes of qualifying for Medicaid depends on whether the Applicant has expressed an intent to return home.

If the Applicant intends to return to his home, regardless of the value of the home, he will not be denied Medicaid benefits because he owns his home. What happens to his home once he dies, is another story. If the home is owned by the Medicaid recipient in his name only, then the state has the right to place a lien on the property for monies spent by the state on his behalf.

This isn't much of a problem if the Applicant is married. Under state and federal law, the Applicant can transfer his home to the Community Spouse without penalty (42 U.S.C. 1396p (c)2A).

If the married Applicant owns his home in his name only, he can transfer the property to his spouse. If he and the Community Spouse own the home jointly, they can sign a deed transferring the home to the Community Spouse. It is important to make the transfer of the joint interest because the property would be in the Applicant's name only in the event the Community Spouse died first.

If the Applicant is too ill to transfer the deed to his spouse, it may be necessary to have the Court appoint a Guardian who will be able to make the transfer.

It is another thing if the Applicant is single. If the Applicant was over 55 when he accepted Medicaid benefits, and the house in his name only, when he dies, the state has the right to place a claim on his Probate Estate for monies spent on his behalf for nursing home care or for home based care or other community based services (42 U.S.C.1396p(b)(B)). Whoever inherits the property will need to reimburse the state for monies spent, or the state can move to force the sale of the property and take the money from the proceeds of the sale of the house.

Most parents want to have their children inherit the one thing the parent has of value, namely their home. If the parent receives Medicaid benefits, there is the chance that the child's inheritance will be reduced if not completely eliminated. This idea is so distressing to some parents that even though they are in good health, they may decide to transfer the homestead to their child with the understanding that the parents will continue to live there for the rest of their lives.

Those planning such a move need to understand that they are trading one risk (need to apply for Medicaid) for several other risks.

⊠ LOSS OF HOMESTEAD CREDITOR PROTECTION

Up to $10,000 of the value of your homestead is protected from creditors during your lifetime. This may not seem like much, but it could keep a roof over your head if the equity in your home is under $10,000. For example, suppose your home is worth $100,000 and you have a mortgage of $90,000. With the exception of property taxes and the loan on your homestead, none of your creditors can force the sale of your property (Civil Practice 5206).

If you simply transfer your homestead to a child, then you lose your homestead protection against creditors. If you are married, then it is a double loss of creditor protection. Not only do you lose creditor protection for yourself, you lose it for your spouse as well (see Page 86).

If the child does not occupy that property as his homestead, then there is no homestead creditor protection whatsoever. The child's creditors can force the sale of the property (that's your home) for relatively small amounts of unpaid debts.

⊠ RISK OF LOSS

Once you transfer the property to your child it becomes his property and that property can be lost or used to pay for his debts just like anything else he owns. Your child could run into serious financial difficulties. Your child could be sued. This is especially a risk if your child is a professional (doctor, nurse, accountant, financial planner, attorney, etc.). If your child is found to be personally liable for damages, then your homestead could become part of the settlement of that law suit.

If your child is (or gets) married, then this complicates matters even more so. If the child divorces, the value of your home might be included as part of the property settlement agreement. This may be to your child's detriment because the child may need to share the value of the property with his/her ex-spouse. If you do not transfer the property, then it cannot become part of his marital equation. Once divorced, your child could be sued for back child or spouse support. A Court could order that your house be sold to pay for monies he owes.

Even if your child is single there is a risk of loss. Your child may want to take out a business loan. It the loan is significant, the lender will want to include everything your child owns as collateral (security for the debt). If the lender learns that you are occupying the house, he will especially want to include your house as collateral because that will give your child motivation to repay the loan.

The point is, transferring your home to your child could be bad for both of you. And that is not the only downside.

⊠   POSSIBLE CAPITAL GAINS TAX

Although Congress has expressed its intent to phase out the Estate Tax, there is no discussion to do away with the Capital Gains Tax. If you gift the property to the child during your lifetime, when he sells the property he will pay a Capital Gains Tax on the increase in value from the price you paid for your home to the selling price at the time your child sells the property.

If you do not make the gift during your lifetime, the child will inherit the property with a step-up in basis, i.e., he will inherit the property at its market value as of the date of your death. Under today's tax structure and continuing until 2009, that step-up in basis is unlimited. If your child sells the property when he inherits it, he will pay no Capital Gains Tax, regardless of how large the step-up in basis. As explained in Chapter 3, in 2010, there will be a limit on the amount that can be inherited free of the Capital Gains Tax but that limit is quite high so for most of us this is not a concern.

⊠ POSSIBLE LOSS OF GOVERNMENT BENEFITS

If you are married and you transfer property to someone other than your spouse, then depending upon the value of the transfer, both you and your spouse could be disqualified from receiving Medicaid or Supplemental Security Income ("SSI") benefits for up to 3 years from the date of transfer of the property. Both you and your spouse could be disqualified for up to 5 years if you transfer the property to an irrevocable Trust. It could happen that during that period of time, one of you takes suddenly ill, say with a stroke. Why jeopardize your right to receive Medicaid for both of you?

Owning a homestead will not disqualify you from receiving Medicaid, but transferring it may make you, and your spouse, ineligible for a long time.

The reader may not be convinced that gifting the house is a bad idea. He may argue "By giving my home to my child, I risk not being able to qualify for Medicaid for three years. If I don't make the gift and need Medicaid at any time during the rest of my lifetime, the state will get the house for sure."

But there are better Estate Plans than the outright gift.

You can give the property to your child, and keep a Life Estate for yourself. Your child will have no right to your homestead while you are alive so you have no fear that the property can be lost or taken from you during your lifetime. Upon your death, your child will own the property 100%, and without the need for Probate. If you receive Medicaid benefits at any time during your life, there can be no recovery from the homestead because all you kept was the right to continue to live in the home during your life time.

Depending on the value of your home, this Life Estate approach might allow you to shorten the Medicaid transfer penalty period, because you are not giving your child the full value of your home, you are just giving away the value of the **Remainder Interest** i.e., what is left of the property after subtracting the value of your life interest.

The value of the Remainder Interest depends on your life expectancy. A gift of a Remainder Interest when you are 90 is worth more to your child than when you are 50.

DETERMINING THE VALUE OF THE REMAINDER INTEREST

The Department of Social Services determines the dollar value of the Remainder Interest by multiplying your life expectancy (expressed as a percentage) by the market value of your home at the time of the transfer.

A Life Estate and Remainder Interest Table is contained in New York State Department of Social Services Administration Directive (96 ADM-8). Local districts may, but are not required to use that table. All the local Department of Social Service need do is to use a "reasonable" method of determining the value of the remainder interest.

A Life Estate is a better Medicaid Qualifying Plan than an outright gift because only a fraction of the value of the home counts as a transfer, but this is not a complete solution because you are still making a lifetime gift. Issues of control and taxes still remain. You will not be able to sell your home without permission from your child. And, as explained on page 37, if you sell the home, you might need to pay a Capital Gains tax.

Before you decide to transfer your home to your child and keep a Life Estate for yourself, it is important to investigate the full tax consequence of the transfer; and then check with an Elder Law attorney to determine the Penalty Period that will be imposed because of the transfer.

TRANSFERRING THE HOME TO A SIBLING

Under state and federal law, if an Applicant owns his home together with a sibling and the sibling lived with the Applicant for at least one year before entering the nursing facility, then the Applicant can transfer the home to the sibling without a Medicaid transfer penalty (42 U.S.C. 1396p). This law presents an opportunity for an unmarried Applicant who has a brother or sister to protect the homestead. The only question is how the sibling becomes co-owner. If the Applicant and his sibling purchased the property together, and the sibling lived in the home for a year prior to the Applicant entering the nursing home, then the sibling's interest in the property is protected. The Applicant can transfer his share of the homestead to his sibling without penalty, and that will protect all of the homestead.

If the house is in the Applicant's name only, then it is important to consult with an Elder Law attorney to determine the best way for the sibling to become part owner of the home. Federal law only requires that the sibling have an *equity interest* in the property. An equity interest could be joint ownership or a Tenancy-In-Common or a Remainder Interest in the homestead. An Elder Law attorney will be able to suggest a method of transferring an equity interest to the sibling that will result in a penalty period of a year or less. The attorney will also assist with preparing documentation to present to DSS to verify that:

> ⇨ the sibling owns an equity interest in the home
> ⇨ the penalty period for the transfer has passed
> ⇨ the sibling occupied the home for a year prior to the Applicant entering the nursing home.

A similar law applies to the Medicaid recipient who owns his home and wants to transfer it to his child. The federal law allows a transfer of the homestead to the child without penalty, provided the child lived with and took care of his parent for at least two years before the parent entered the nursing home.

There is no requirement that the child own an equity interest in the property; but the federal statute does require that the state verify that the child lived in the home and provided care to the parent for the two years; and that this care enabled the parent to remain at home rather than be placed in a nursing home (42 U.S.C. 1396p(c)(2)(A)(iv)).

Because there is a two year qualification period, it may be just as easy to transfer the home to the child and wait out the two years. That is certainly the case if the home is worth less than the two year penalty in your county. As explained on page 201, the average cost of nursing care currently ranges from $5,393 to $8,272.

$$\$5,393 \times 24 = \$129,432$$
$$\$8,272 \times 24 = \$198,528$$

But if the home is worth significantly more, then it is important to consult with an Elder Law attorney, preferably prior to the two year period. The attorney may suggest that parent and child sign a Caretaker's Agreement that sets out the terms and conditions of the transfer; i.e., what care the child promises to give to the parent over the next two years in exchange for the transfer of the homestead to the child.

The attorney will explain how to document that care over the two year period so that the information can be presented to DSS when the parent applies for Medicaid.

CAUTION   DON'T TRY THIS ON YOUR OWN

A Medicaid Qualifying Plan is not something to attempt on your own. The Medicaid program is complex and volatile. There are four levels of laws that govern Medicaid. There are the federal statutes (Social Security Act Title XIX/P.L. 89-97); and the U.S. Code of Federal Regulations (42 CFR 430-435) that say how the federal statutes are to be administered in the United States. There are state Medicaid statutes (The Social Services Law: Title II Medical Assistance for Needy Persons); and the Title 18 of the New York Code, Rules & Regulations (NYCRR) that determine how the Medicaid program is to be administered in the state of New York. These four levels of law are constantly changing, often with little or no notice to the general public.

And increasingly, laws are being passed with built in obsolescence. That is the case with the Estate Tax law. As explained on page 50, Estate Taxes are being phased out, but only until 2011 when they are scheduled to be reinstated.

State law is moving in that direction as well. For example, much of this chapter was based on New York Social Services Law 366. You can download this statute from the Internet. It is so lengthy that you will need at least 35 sheets of paper to do so. Not only is statute 366 lengthy and complex, but it has built in obsolescence. Specifically, many parts of the statute have footnotes explaining that a given section of the statute will no longer be in effect upon a certain date; for example:

        Section 4 (j) expires June 30, 2003,
        Section 4 (k) expires July 1, 2003
        Section 4 (u) (1) expires March 31, 2002, etc.

In addition to the fact that the law is constantly changing, there is the problem of Court challenges to the law. Certain sections of Social Services Law 366 are currently in limbo until the matter is settled in Court. The footnote to Section 10 (a) of the statute explains:

> The constitutionality of certain line item vetoes by Governor Pataki in 1998 is the subject of pending litigation (SHELDON SILVER, MEMBER AND SPEAKER, NEW YORK STATE ASSEMBLY V. GEORGE E. PATAKI, GOVERNOR, STATE OF NEW YORK, Misc.2d, NYLJ. Jan. 14, 1999). The New York State Legislature Bill Drafting Commission will carry the affected provisions of the law as they appear in the event the vetoes are finally upheld judicially and as they would appear if such vetoes are finally held to be unconstitutional.

To make matters worse, the Medicaid program is not uniformly administered within the state. This is the case for the Spousal Refusal option. Whether or not DSS decides to enforce the right of the state to demand payment from the Community Spouse, depends on the current practice in that county. Some counties have sued for monies owed. Many counties have not.

And what may be an acceptable Medicaid qualifying option in one county, may be challenged by DSS in another county. If the Department of Social Services decides to challenge a particular strategy, even though that strategy is based on federal or state law, you will have no choice but to appeal the ruling.

THE MEDICAID APPEAL PROCESS

The first step in the appeal process is an administrative hearing at the Department of Social Services office. The hearing officer is an attorney employed by New York State Department of Health. This administrative procedure is called a "Fair Hearing." The hearing officer will determine whether DSS has correctly applied the rules in determining the Applicant's eligibility.

If the hearing officer decides in favor of the DSS, then the next step in the appeals process is to bring the case before the New York Supreme Court (Civil Practice Law & Rules 5701). The judge of the Supreme Court will take a broader look at the picture and consider state and federal law, as well as your Constitutional rights under the law. If you are turned down in the state Court, you can appeal to a federal court — all the way up to the United States Supreme Court.

The appeal process is expensive, stressful and time consuming. It may be better to choose a strategy that the Department of Social Services office in that county has allowed in the past, even if it is not the very best Qualifying Plan for you.

For example, on page 199 we explained it was the legal right of the Community Spouse to ask the Department of Social Services to allow her to keep enough assets to generate the minimum monthly income as required by both state and federal law.

It is reasonable to ask DSS to allow her to keep as much of her assets as is necessary to achieve that income, even if it means keeping more than allowed as a resource allowance. But it will take the assistance of an experienced Elder Law attorney to convince the Department of Social Services that allowing her to keep more in resources is a proper thing to do. No doubt DSS will deny the request and it will be necessary to go through an Appeals process to decide the issue. The appeals process can drag on for months. Meanwhile, the status of the Applicant remains in limbo.

Because of the legal cost of the Appeal and the uncertainty of whether the Court will agree that additional resources are necessary for the support of the Community Spouse, it may be better to use a different strategy that will generate income to her. As we discussed there are several strategies available to the Community Spouse; from keeping her excess resources to generate more income (spousal refusal) to paying off all of her debts. Paying off her debts will not give her additional income, but it will leave her with more spendable income each month.

The goal is to get the Applicant qualified for Medicaid as quickly as possible, and with the least amount of cost and hassle. An experienced Elder Law attorney can explain what strategies have been allowed in the past in your county and which strategies are likely to be challenged.

The key word is "experienced." Before employing an attorney, determine what percentage of his practice is devoted to Medicaid eligibility; how long he has practiced Elder Law in that county; and whether he is familiar with the appeals process, should the need arise.

Guiding Those You Love 11

Once you are satisfied with your Estate Plan, then the final thing to consider is whether your heirs will be able to locate your assets after you're gone.

Most people have their business records in one place, their Will in another place, car titles and deeds in still another place. When someone dies, their beneficiaries may feel as if they are playing a game of "hide and seek" with the decedent. The game might be fun were it not for the fact that unlocated items may be forever lost. For example, suppose you die in an accident and no one knows you are insured by your credit card company for accidental death in the amount of $25,000. The only one to profit is the insurance company, which is just that much richer because no one told them that you died as a result of an accident.

And how about a key to a safe deposit box? Will anyone find it? Even if they find the key, how will they locate the box?

It is not difficult to arrange things so that your affairs are always in order. It amounts to being aware of what you own (and owe) and keeping a record of your possessions. A side benefit is that by doing so, you will always know where all your business records are. If you ever spent time trying to collect information to file your taxes or trying to find a lost stock or bond certificate, you will appreciate the value of organizing your records.

ORGANIZING YOUR RECORDS

Heirs need all the help they can get. It is difficult enough dealing with the loss, without the frustration of trying to locate important documents. Your heirs will have no problem locating your assets if you keep all of your records in a single place. It can be a desk drawer or a file cabinet or even a shoe box. It is helpful if you keep a separate file or folder for each type of investment. You might consider setting up the following folders:

📁 THE BANK & SECURITIES FOLDER

Store your original certificates for stocks, bonds, mutual funds, certificates of deposit, in a folder labeled BANK & SECURITIES FOLDER. In addition to the original certificate include a copy of the contract you signed with each financial institution. The contract will show where you have funds and who you named as beneficiary or joint owner of the account. If someone owes you money and has signed a promissory note or mortgage that identifies you as the lender, then you can store these documents in this folder as well.

If you wish to store your original documents in a safe deposit box, then keep a record of the location of the safe deposit box, and the number of the box, in this folder. Make a copy of all of the items stored in the box and place the copies in this folder. If you have an extra key to the box, then put the key in the folder. If you are the only person with access to the box, it may take a Probate procedure to remove items from the box once you die. Consider allowing someone you trust to be able to gain entry to the box in the event of your incapacity or death.

🗁 THE INSURANCE FOLDER

The INSURANCE FOLDER is for each original insurance policy that you own, be it car insurance, homeowner's insurance or a health care insurance policy. If you purchased real property, you may have received a title commitment at closing and the original title insurance policy some weeks later when you received your original deed from recording. If you cannot locate the title insurance policy, then contact the closing agent and have them send you a copy of your title insurance policy.

🗁 THE PENSION AND ANNUITY FOLDER

Put all of the documents relating to your pension or annuity in this folder. Include the telephone number and/or address of the person to contact in the event of your death.

FOR FEDERAL RETIREES

If you are a Federal Retiree, you should have received your **PERSONAL IDENTIFICATION NUMBER (PIN)** and the person who will inherit your pension (your *survivor annuitant*) should have received his/her own PIN as well. It is relatively simple to obtain this during your lifetime, but it may be difficult and/or stressful for your survivor annuitant to work through the system once you are gone.

Survivor annuitant benefits are not automatic. Your survivor annuitant must apply for them by submitting a death claim to the Office of Personnel Management. Your survivor needs to know that it is necessary to apply and also how to apply. You can call Office of Personal Management at (888) 767-6738 to get printed information that you can keep in this file to guide your survivor annuitant through the process.

🗁 THE DEED FOLDER

Many people save every scrap of paper associated with the closing of real property. If you closed recently on real estate and there was a mortgage involved in the purchase, you probably walked away from closing with enough paper to wallpaper your kitchen. If you wish, you can keep all of those papers in a separate file that identifies the property, for example:

CLOSING PAPERS FOR THE SYRACUSE CONDO

Place the original deed (or a copy if the original is in a safe deposit box) in a separate DEED FOLDER. Include cemetery deeds, condominium deeds, timesharing certificates, deed to out of state property, etc. Also include a copy of related documents such as an Abstract of Title, or a recorded condominium approval. If you have a title insurance policy, put the original in the insurance folder, and a copy in this folder. If you have a mortgage on your property, put a copy of the recorded mortgage and promissory note in a separate LIABILITY FOLDER.

LOCATING REAL PROPERTY

If you own a vacant lot, your beneficiaries will find the deed (or a copy) in this folder but that deed will not contain the address of that property because it doesn't have one. The post office does not assign a street address until there is a building on the site. Your beneficiaries can get the location of the property from city or county records. But why make things hard for them? Include a handwritten note in this folder that tells them exactly how to locate the property.

THE TAX RECORD FOLDER

Your Personal Representative (or next of kin) will need to file your final income tax returns. Keep a copy of your tax returns (both federal and state) for the past three years in your Tax Record Folder. As explained in Chapter 3, beginning in 2010, there will be a cap on the step-up basis to 4.3 million dollars for property inherited by your spouse and 1.3 million for property inherited by anyone else. It is important to keep a record of the basis of your property, not only for your heirs, but yourself should you decide to sell the property during your lifetime. If you purchase real property, you need to keep a record of the purchase price as well as monies you paid to improve the property. You need these records to determine whether a Capital Gains Tax is due on the transfer. Your accountant can help you set up a bookkeeping system to keep a running record of your basis in everything you own of value.

THE LIABILITY FOLDER

The LIABILITY FOLDER should contain all loan documents of debts that you owe. For example, if you purchased real property and have a mortgage on that property, put a copy of the mortgage and promissory note in this folder. If you owe money on a car, put the loan documents in this folder. A lease is a liability, because you have contracted to pay a certain amount for the period of the lease, so include a copy of any lease agreement in this folder.

If you have a credit card, put a copy of the contract you signed with the credit card company in this folder. Many people never take the time to calculate their net worth (what a person owns less what that person owes). By having a record of your assets and outstanding debts, you can calculate your net worth whenever you wish.

⬜ THE PERSONAL PROPERTY FOLDER

MOTOR VEHICLES

Put all motor vehicle titles in a Personal Property folder. This includes cars, mobile homes, boats, planes, etc. If you owe money on the vehicle, the lender may have possession of the title certificate. If such is the case, then put a copy of the title certificate and registration in this folder and a copy of the loan documents in a separate liability folder. If you own a boat or plane, then identify the location of the motor vehicle. For example, if you are leasing space in an airplane hangar or in a marina, keep a copy of the leasing agreement in this file.

JEWELRY

If you own expensive jewelry, keep a picture of the item together with the sales receipt or written appraisal in this folder.

COLLECTOR'S ITEMS

If you own a valuable art or coin collection, or any other item of significant value, include a picture of the item in this file. Also include evidence of ownership of the item, such as a sales receipt or a certificate of authenticity, or a written appraisal of the property.

⬜ THE PERSONAL RECORDS FOLDER

The PERSONAL RECORDS FOLDER should include documents that relate to you personally, such as a birth certificate, naturalization papers, marriage certificate, divorce papers, military records, social security card; etc.

THE ESTATE PLANNING DOCUMENT FOLDER

WILL/TRUST

Place your Will and/or Trust in a separate folder. If your attorney has your original Will, then make a note of that fact together with a copy of the Will. If the original document is in a safe deposit box, then place a copy of the document in this folder together with instructions about how to find the original.

It is important to keep a copy of your Will or Trust because over the years you may forget what provision you made. Keeping a copy in your home may save you the time and effort to retrieve the document, just to determine whether it needs to be updated.

PRENUPTIAL/POSTNUPTIAL AGREEMENT

Prenuptial or postnuptial agreements usually provide for the disposition of your property upon your death, so a copy of the agreement should be included in this folder.

OTHER ESTATE PLANNING DOCUMENTS

You can include the original or a copy of your Health Care Proxy, Durable Power of Attorney, or Preneed Funeral Plan in this folder.

THE QUICK-FIND FOLDER

Many do not have the time, nor inclination, to "play" with all these folders. They do not anticipate an immediate demise. Getting hit by a truck, or dying in a fiery plane crash is not something to think about, much less prepare for. But consider that death is not the only problem. You could take suddenly ill (say with a stroke) and become incapacitated. Even the most time-starved optimist should have a murmur of concern that his loved ones will be left with a mess should something unforeseen happen.

If you do not feel like doing a complete job of organizing your records at this time, consider an abridged version. You can set up a single folder and place all of your important papers in that folder. You need to make the folder easily accessible to whoever you wish to manage your affairs in the event of your incapacity or death. You can do this by letting that person know of the existence of the folder and how to get it in an emergency.

You can keep the folder in an easily accessed place in your home with the folder identified as containing important papers. We labeled it "THE QUICK-FIND FOLDER" because the folder gives you and your family easy access to important information and/or documents. But you can create your own heading such as: "MY IMPORTANT PAPERS" or if you want a particular person to access the file, you might label it: "RECORDS FOR MY SON, ROBERT"

It is helpful if you include a list of all you own and the location of each item in that folder. There is a form that you can use on the next page to assist with your organization of your important papers.

THE QUICK FIND FOLDER

FINANCIAL RECORDS

BANK
Name and address of Bank, Account Number,

_____

_____

Location of Safe Deposit Box and Key

_____

SECURITIES
Identity and location of stocks and bonds:

_____

_____

Name, Telephone number of securities broker

_____

INSURANCE POLICIES
Name of Company, Location of Policy, Insurance Agent

_____

_____

PENSIONS/ANNUITIES

_____

NAME OF CONTACT PERSON _____

IF FEDERAL RETIREE: PIN NUMBER: _____

TAX RECORDS
LOCATION_____
Name, Telephone number of accountant

_____

PROPERTY RECORDS
TITLE TO MOTOR VEHICLES _____
DEEDS _____
MORTGAGES _____

LIABILITY RECORD

MORTGAGES_____

LEASES _____

PROMISSORY NOTES_____

CREDIT CARDS _____

LOCATION OF LEGAL DOCUMENTS

BIRTH CERTIFICATE AND/OR NATURALIZATION PAPERS

_____

PASSPORT _____

MARRIAGE CERTIFICATE _____

DIVORCE DECREE _____

ARMED SERVICE DISCHARGE PAPERS

_____

LOCATION OF ESTATE PLANNING DOCUMENTS

WILL _____

TRUST _____

PRENUPTIAL/POSTNUPTIAL AGREEMENT

_____

HEALTH CARE DIRECTIVE _____

POWER OF ATTORNEY _____

PRENEED FUNERAL PLAN _____

ATTORNEY
Name, Telephone number   _____

_____

We discussed people's natural disinclination to make an Estate Plan until they are faced with their own mortality. Many believe that they will make just one Will and then die (maybe that's why they put off making a Will). The reality is, most people who make a Will change it at least once before they die. If you have an Estate Plan, it is important to update it when any of the following events take place:

✍ CHANGE IN MARITAL STATUS

If your marry or divorce, there are certain changes that take place by law. For example, if you divorce and then die before you get around to changing your Will or Trust, then any provision that you made for your ex-spouse in the document will be read as if your ex-spouse died before you (Estates 5-1.4).

But it is important to not just rely on the law. Best to change all documents after a divorce or separation. This includes your Health Care Proxy, Durable Power of Attorney, deeds, insurance policies, etc.

NOTIFY EMPLOYER OF CHANGE

If you change your marital status (either marry or divorce) you need to tell your employer of the change so that the employer can change your status for purposes of paycheck tax deductions. If you have a health insurance plan or a pension plan, that provides benefits to your spouse, then these need to be changed as well.

✍ A CHANGE IN RELATIONSHIP

Getting married, separated or divorced; having a child; having a beneficiary of your Estate die, these are all profound changes in one's life. When the dust settles, it is important to examine your Estate Plan to see if it needs revision. If you have a Trust you can change it by having your attorney prepare an amendment to the Trust. You can change your Will by adding a *codicil* (a supplement) to the Will.

If you decide that your Will needs a complete revision, then it is important to have a new Will prepared. If you simply rip up the old Will, that will effectively revoke the Will. But it could happen that someone (perhaps your attorney) has a copy of the Will. If no one knows that you revoked the Will, they may think the Will is lost and then offer the copy of the Will for Probate. If you draft a new Will, then the first paragraph should say, "I revoke all prior Wills ..." This makes it clear that you want the new Will to replace all other Wills.

 NEW SPOUSE OR CHILD CAN
CHALLENGE OLD WILL

CHALLENGE BY SURVIVING SPOUSE

If you marry and "forget" to change the Will you prepared prior to your marriage, then your spouse is entitled to take his/her Elective Share of your Net Estate (see Page 47). The beneficiaries of your Estate will need to contribute a proportionate share of their inheritance to make up that Elective Share (Estates 5-1.1 A).

CHALLENGE BY AFTERBORN CHILD

A child born after you prepared your Will is entitled to receive as much as you give to any of your other children:

NO PROVISION FOR ANY CHILD

If you had one or more children when you made your Will and you made no provision for any of your children in that Will, then any child born to you after you made the Will is not entitled to share in your Estate either.

PROVISION MADE FOR OTHER CHILD

If you made a gift to one or more of your children and a child is born after the Will, then the afterborn child has the right to share in the gift made to your other children. For example, if you made a gift of $50,000 to your child, then a child born to you after you made your Will is entitled to share equally in that gift; i.e., each child gets $25,000. But if it appears from the Will that you intended the $50,000 to go to your living child only, then the afterborn child is entitled to inherit as much of your Probate Estate as he/she would have inherited under New York's Rules of Intestate Succession.

NO CHILD LIVING AT TIME OF WILL

If you no children when you made your Will, any child born after the Will is entitled to inherit as much of your Probate Estate as if you died without a Will. The beneficiaries of your Will will need to contribute as much as necessary to make up that intestate share (Estates 5-3.2).

As you can see the laws relating to an afterborn child are complex; and could lead to disagreements and hard feelings for those forced to contribute to the child's share. It is better that you change your Will when a child is born so that your child receives no more and no less than you intended.

✍ BENEFICIARY MOVES OR DIES

Most people remember to name an alternate beneficiary should one of their beneficiaries die. But how many of us remember to notify the pension plan or insurance company when a beneficiary moves?

It is important that your beneficiary's address be available to those in charge of distributing funds upon your death. Many life insurance proceeds are never paid because the company cannot locate the beneficiary. The Actuarial Office of the Federal Employees' Group Life Insurance Program reported that as of October, 2001, they had over 40 million dollars in unpaid benefits, mostly because they could not locate the beneficiary at the last given address.

✍ RELOCATION TO A NEW STATE OR COUNTRY

There is no need to change your Estate Plan for a move within the state of New York. If your attorney has your original Will or any other original of your Estate Planning documents, you may want to retrieve these items and take them with you to the new location if you are moving a significant distance from your present location, or out of state.

There is much to check out if you move to another state or country. If you have a Will, you need to determine whether your Will conforms to the laws of the state of your new residence. Most states will honor a Will drafted according to New York law, however, the rights of a spouse vary considerably state to state. If you are married and have not provided the minimum amount as required by the laws of the new state, then should you die before your spouse, your Will may be challenged on that basis.

The same applies to a Trust. Most states allow a surviving spouse to demand funds from the Trust of the decedent spouse, if he did not provide the minimum amount to his spouse as required by the laws of that state.

LAWS OF INTESTATE SUCCESSION

If you do not have a Will, then it is important to check out the Laws of Intestate Succession for that state. In some states they are referred to as the *Laws of Descent and Distribution*. Each state has its own laws relating to the inheritance of property and those laws are very different from each other. Who has the right to inherit your property in the state of New York may be different from who can inherit your property in another state. If you do not have a Will, then this is the time to think about who will get your property in the state of your new residence.

This is especially important for those who are married. The right of a spouse to inherit property varies significantly from state to state. There is a world of difference between the rights of a spouse in a community property state (Arizona, California, Idaho, Louisiana, New Mexico, Nevada, Texas, Washington and Wisconsin) and other states. There is even variation in the rights of a spouse from one community property state to another!

CREDITOR PROTECTION

Creditor protection is another item that is significantly different state to state. If you have much debt, then determine what items can be inherited by your family free of your debts.

TAX CONSIDERATIONS

You need to check out the taxes of the new state. Each state has its own tax structure. Some states have an inheritance tax, or a transfer tax on all inherited property. If state taxes are high, you may need an Estate Plan that will minimize the impact of those taxes.

OTHER ESTATE PLANNING DOCUMENTS

If you have a Health Care Proxy, then you need to determine whether this document will be honored in the new state. Many states have laws directing physicians to honor a Health Care Directive that is properly drafted in another state. But even if the laws of the state honor your New York Proxy, consider drafting another in the new state. Health Care Directives vary significantly state to state. Other states may have laws that enable you to appoint someone with powers similar to a Health Care Agent, but the laws of the state may refer to such person as a *Patient Advocate* or a *Health Care Surrogate* or a *Health Care Representative.* It is best to sign a new Health Care Directive using the form and terminology recognized in the new state, rather than chance any confusion should you become ill and find yourself in an emergency situation.

Similarly, if you have appointed someone to handle your finances under a Durable Power of Attorney, you may want to have another prepared in conformity with the laws of the new state, so there will be no question of the right of your Attorney-In-Fact to conduct business on your behalf.

RELOCATING THE MEDICAID RECIPIENT

If you are married to a Medicaid recipient, and you, and/or the recipient, plan to move to another state, you need to check out whether he will continue to be eligible in that state. As explained in the previous chapter, Medicaid is both a state and federal program. Once a person qualifies for Medicaid in one state, he can be transferred to another state; provided he qualifies under that state's Medicaid program.

For example, New York does not have an upper limit for income. Some other states do. If an Applicant has an income that exceeds the limit in a state that has an *income cap*, then the Applicant may be refused Medicaid benefits in that state. If you plan to move a Medicaid recipient to another state, it is important to apply for Medicaid before the move and have a written acceptance into the Medicaid program. If the Medicaid Agency in that state says that the New York Medicaid recipient does not meet their state requirements for eligibility, then check with an Elder Law attorney to learn what options are available to allow the recipient to qualify for Medicaid in that state.

As you can see, state law has an important impact on your Estate Plan. When moving to another state, it is important to either educate yourself about the laws of the state, or to consult with an attorney who can assist you in reviewing your Estate Plan to see if that plan will accomplish your goals in that state.

✍ A SIGNIFICANT CHANGE IN THE LAW

We pay our legislators (state and federal) to make laws and, if necessary, change those in effect. We pay judges to interpret the law and that interpretation may change the way the law operates. The legislature and the judiciary do their job and so laws change frequently. Tax laws are particularly volatile. The 2001 change in the Federal Estate Tax law gradually increases the Exclusion amount so that by 2010 no Federal Estate Tax will be due regardless of the value of your Estate.

You may be thinking that there is no need for an Estate Tax plan because you don't intend to die prior to 2010. But any certainty relating to death and taxes is false security (especially taxes, in this case). As explained in Chapter 2, the law as passed in 2001, is effective only until December 31, 2010. If lawmakers do nothing, then on January 1, 2011, the Federal Estate Tax goes back into effect; and Estates that exceed one million dollars will once again be subject to Estate taxes.

And that is not the only uncertainty. Each state has its own Estate Tax structure. It remains to be seen how each state will react to the federal change. Some states may follow the lead of the federal government and increase their Estate Tax Exclusion in the same manner. Other states may see this as an opportunity to "pick up the slack" i.e., to increase their Estate Taxes, so that monies that would have been paid to the federal government will now be paid to the state. You need to keep up with the news to learn about changes in the law that affect your Estate Plan. It is a good idea to check with your attorney on a regular basis to see if any change in the state or federal law affects your current Estate plan. And also check out the Eagle Publishing Company Web site for changes we will post to keep this book fresh.   http://www.eaglepublishing.com

SPRING CLEANING YOUR RECORDS

Used to be, that housewives did a once a year, floor to ceiling, "spring housecleaning." We know of no survey telling whether today's houseperson conducts an annual purge of dirt and clutter. We suspect it went by the wayside when housewives entered the work force as full time employees. But it was a good practice. In many cases, it was the only time of the year when the house was truly clean and tidy. It is a good idea to incorporate that old-fashioned housecleaning practice to your financial records and clean them up on a regular basis. There is no need to keep the deed to real property that you have long since sold; a lease agreement to an apartment you no longer rent; a credit card to a closed account, etc.

Many hesitate to toss out some scrap of paper for fear it will not be available for future reference. There are documents you may need to keep for a lengthy period of time to establish a basis for tax purposes. You can avoid the problem of keeping too much, or not enough, by taking your box (or folder) of records with you the next time you visit with your accountant or attorney. You can ask your advisor to help you organize your records and assist with your "housecleaning."

Keys are another item to keep up to date. You may keep keys for sentimental reasons, but there is no business reason to keep a key to a car you no longer own, a safe deposit box you no longer lease, etc. Keeping such keys can only cause confusion should you become disabled or die. Whoever takes possession of your property will be left with mysterious keys. He will probably think the keys are protecting something of value. Unless you enjoy picturing his frustration as he seeks an imaginary treasure, pitch the key.

Glossary

ACTUARIAL TABLE An *actuarial table* is a table organized according to statistical data that indicates the life expectancy of a person.

ADMINISTRATION The *administration* of a Probate Estate is the management and settlement of the decedent's affairs. There are different types of administration.

AGENT   An *agent* is someone who is authorized by another (the principal) to act for, or in place of, the principal.

AMENDMENT   An *amendment* to a Trust is an addition to the Trust that changes the provisions of the Trust.

ANATOMICAL GIFT   An *anatomical gift* is the donation of all or part of the body of the decedent for a specified purpose, such as transplantation or research.

ANNUITANT   An *annuitant* is someone who is entitled to receive payments under an annuity contract.

ANNUITY CONTRACT An *annuity contract* is a contract that gives someone (the annuitant) the right to receive periodic payments (monthly, quarterly) for the life of the annuitant or for a given number of years.

ASSET An *asset* is anything owned by someone that has a value, including personal property (jewelry, paintings, securities, cash, motor vehicles, etc.) and real property (condominiums, vacant lots, acreage, residences, etc.)

ATTORNEY or ATTORNEY AT LAW An *attorney*, also known as an *Attorney at law*, or a *lawyer*, is someone who is licensed by the state to practice law in that state.

ATTORNEY-IN-FACT An *Attorney-In-Fact* is someone appointed to act as an Agent for another (the Principal) under a Power of Attorney.

BASIS The *basis* is a value that is assigned to an asset for the purpose of determining the gain (or loss) on the sale of the item or in determining the value of the item in the hands of someone who has received it as a gift.

BENEFICIARY A *beneficiary* is one who benefits from the acts of another person. In this book, we refer to a beneficiary as one who inherits property from the decedent.

BY REPRESENTATION   *By Representation* is a method of distributing an inheritance to a group of people such that if one of them dies before the transfer is made, the share intended for that person is divided equally between his surviving lineal descendants in the generation nearest to him.

CAPITAL GAINS TAX A *Capital Gains tax* is a tax on the increase in the basis of property sold by a taxpayer.

CHARITABLE REMAINDER ANNUITY TRUST   A *Charitable Remainder Annuity Trust* is a Trust that is required to make payments on a regular basis (monthly, quarterly, etc.) to a designated person (the Annuitant) for a certain period of time or until his death. Once the annuity is paid, whatever remains in the Trust is donated to a tax exempt charity.

CLAIM A *claim* against the decedent's Estate is a demand for payment. To be effective, the claim must be filed with the Probate court within the time limits set by law.

CLOSE CORPORATION A *Close Corporation* is a corporation whose voting shares are held by a single shareholder or a closely-knit group of shareholders.

CODICIL A *codicil* to a Will is an addition to the Will that changes or replaces certain parts of the Will.

COLUMBARIUM A *columbarium* is a vault with niches (spaces) for urns that contain the ashes of cremated bodies.

CORPORATION *Corporation* is a company created by one or more persons according to the laws of the state. The company is owned by the *shareholders* or *stockholders*. Each owner has limited liability (see Limited Liability).

CUSTODIAN A *Custodian* under the *New York Uniform Transfers to Minors Act* is a person or a financial institution that accepts responsibility for the care and management of property given to a minor child.

DECEDENT The *decedent* is the person who died.

DESCENDANT A *descendant* is someone who descends from a common ancestor. There are two kinds of descendants: a *lineal descendant* and a *collateral descendant*. The lineal descendant is one who descends in a straight line such as father to son to grandson. The collateral descendant is one who descends in a parallel line, such as a cousin. In this book, unless otherwise stated, the term *descendant* refers to a *lineal descendant*. The word *issue* has the same meaning as the word descendant.

DISTRIBUTION The *distribution* of a Trust Estate or of a Probate Estate is the giving to the beneficiary that part of the Estate to which the beneficiary is entitled.

DURABLE As used in the Power of Attorney, the word ***durable*** means that the Power of Attorney will remain, in effect in the event that the principal (the person giving the Power of Attorney) becomes incapacitated.

ELECTIVE SHARE The ***Elective Share*** is the minimum amount of the decedent's Estate that a surviving spouse is entitled to receive under law. In New York that amount is $50,000 or 1/3 of the decedent's Net Estate, whichever is greater.

ENTITLEMENT An ***entitlement*** is a right to receive some benefit income or property.

EQUITY INTEREST An ***equity interest*** is an ownership interest. It is the value of the ownership interest over and above monies owed on the property.

ESTATE A person's ***Estate*** is all of the property (both real and personal property) owned by that person. A person's Estate is also referred to as his ***Taxable Estate*** because all of the decedent's assets must be included when determining whether any Estate taxes are due when the person dies. Compare to ***Probate Estate***.

EXECUTOR An ***Executor*** is someone appointed by a Will maker to carry out the directions and requests in his Will.

FACE VALUE The ***face value*** of a life insurance policy is the value stated on the insurance certificate or policy. It is the amount payable upon the death of the insured person.

FIDUCIARY A ***fiduciary*** is one who holds property in Trust for another or one who acts for the benefit of another.

GRANTEE The *Grantee* of a deed (also called the party of the second part) named in a deed is the person who receives title to the property from the grantor.

GRANTOR A *Grantor* is someone who transfers property. The Grantor of a deed, (also called the party of the first part), is the person who transfers property to a new owner (the *Grantee*). The Grantor of a Trust is someone who creates the Trust and then transfers property into the Trust. Also see *Settlor*.

GUARANTOR A *Guarantor* is someone who promises to pay a debt or perform a contract for another in the event that person does not fulfill his obligation.

GUARDIAN A *Guardian* is someone who has legal authority to care for the person or property of a minor or for someone who has been found by the court to be incapacitated.

HEALTH CARE AGENT A *Health Care Agent* is someone who is appointed by another (the *Principal)* to make medical decisions on behalf of the Principal, in the event that the Principal is to too ill to speak for himself.

HEALTH CARE PROXY   A *Health Care Proxy* is a document in which a person appoints someone to serve as his Health Care Agent.

HEIR   An *heir* is someone who is entitled to inherit the decedent's property in the event that the decedent dies without a Will. This includes the surviving spouse as well as the state of New York, if the decedent had no surviving relative.

HOMESTEAD The *homestead* is the dwelling that is owned, and occupied, in the state of New York, as the owner's principal residence.

INCAPACITATED   The term *incapacitated* is used in two ways. A person is *physically incapacitated* if he lacks the ability to care for himself in some way. A person is *legally incapacitated* if a court finds that a person is unable to care for his person or property. Once the Court determines that a person is legally incapacitated, the judge will appoint someone to care for the person or property of the incapacitated person.

INTER VIVOS TRUST   An *Inter Vivos Trust* (also known as a *Living Trust*) is a Trust that is created and becomes effective during the lifetime of the Settlor (or Grantor) as contrasted with a Trust that the Settlor includes as part of his Will to take effect upon his death.

INTESTATE *Intestate* means not having a Will or dying without a Will. *Testate* is to have a Will or dying with a Will.

IRREVOCABLE CONTRACT An *irrevocable contract* is a contract that cannot be revoked, withdrawn, or cancelled by any of the parties to that contract.

IRREVOCABLE TRUST   An *Irrevocable Trust* is a Trust that cannot be cancelled. It cannot be terminated until its purpose is accomplished.

IRREVOCABLE INSURANCE TRUST   An *Irrevocable Insurance Trust* is a Trust that is set up to purchase life insurance. The proceeds of the life insurance policy can be used to pay taxes that may be due upon the death of the insured person.

ISSUE See DESCENDANT.

KEY MAN INSURANCE *Key man insurance* is an insurance policy designed to protect a company from economic loss in the event that an important employee of the company becomes disabled or dies.

LAWS OF INTESTATE SUCCESSION The *Laws of Intestate Succession (*also known as the *Laws of Descent and Distribution*) are the laws of the state that determine who is to inherit the decedent's Probate Estate if the decedent died without a valid Will.

LEGALESE *Legalese* refers to the use of legal terms and confusing text used by many attorneys to draft legal documents.

LIFE ESTATE A *Life Estate* interest in real property is the right to possess and occupy that property for so long as the holder of the Life Estate lives.

LIMITED LIABILITY *Limited Liability* as related to a corporation or other company created according to state law, means that a shareholder of the company is not personally responsible to pay the debts of the company beyond the amount that he/she invested in the company. The shareholder can be held liable for unlawful or negligent acts done while conducting company business.

LIMITED LIABILITY COMPANY A *Limited Liability Company* is a company created according to the laws of the state, to conduct business or for any other lawful purpose. All of the members of the company have limited liability.

LIMITED PARTNERSHIP A *Limited Partnership* is a partnership created according to the laws of the state. Each *Limited Partner* has limited liability. Each *General Partner* is personally liable for all of the debts of the company. (See Limited Liability).

LITIGATION *Litigation* is the process of carrying on a lawsuit, i.e., to sue for some right or remedy in a court of law. A Litigation Attorney is one who is experienced in conducting the law suit and in particular, going to trial.

LIVING WILL A *Living Will* gives instructions to the physician about whether life support systems should be withheld or withdrawn in the event that the person who signs the Living Will is terminally ill or in a persistent vegetative state and unable to speak for himself.

MEDICAID *Medicaid* is a public assistance program sponsored jointly by the federal and state government to provide medical care for people with low income and limited resources.

NET ESTATE The *Net Estate* is defined by New York law to be the decedent's Probate Estate less funeral expenses, administrative expenses, and valid claims. It also includes non Probate transfers such as property held in the decedent's Trust, or in a joint account; as well as property gifted by the decedent at any time during his marriage for the benefit of anyone other than the surviving spouse.

NET WORTH A person's *net worth* is the value of all of the property that he owns less what he owes.

NEXT OF KIN   *Next of kin* has two meanings in law: *next of kin* can refer to a person's nearest blood relation or it can refer to those people (not necessarily blood relations) who are entitled to inherit the property of the decedent if the decedent died without a will.

PARTNERSHIP   A business *partnership* is an agreement between two or more persons to use their assets and/or services to carry on a business for profit as co-owners.

PERSONAL EFFECTS *Personal effects* is property that is owned for one's personal use such as clothing, jewelry, books, and other items generally found in the one's home.

PERSONAL PROPERTY *Personal property* is all property owned by a person that is not real property (real estate). It includes personal effects, cars, securities, bank accounts, insurance policies, etc.

PERSONAL REPRESENTATIVE   The *Personal Representative* is someone appointed by the Surrogate's Court to settle the decedent's Estate and to distribute whatever is left to the proper beneficiary.

PETITION A *Petition* is a formal written request to a Court asking the Court to take action or issue an order on a given matter; e.g. a request to appoint a Guardian.

POST-NUPTIAL AGREEMENT   A *Post-nuptial agreement* is an agreement made by a couple after marriage to decide their respective rights in case of a dissolution or the death of a spouse.

POWER OF ATTORNEY A *Power of Attorney* is a document in which someone (the *Principal*) gives another (his *Agent*) authority to do specific things on behalf of the Principal.

PRE-NUPTIAL AGREEMENT A *pre-nuptial agreement* (also known as an *antenuptial agreement*) is an agreement made prior to marriage whereby a couple determines how their property is to be managed during their marriage and how their property is to be divided should one die, or they later divorce.

PRINCIPAL OF A POWER OF ATTORNEY   The *Principal* of a Power of Attorney is someone who gives another (his *Agent*) authority to act on his (the Principal's) behalf.

PRINCIPAL OF A TRUST   The *Principal* of a Trust is the Trust property. The Trust income is the monies that are earned on the Trust Principal.

PROBABLE CAUSE   *Probable cause* exists if it is reasonable to believe certain facts. Mere suspicion is not enough. For probable cause to exist, there must be more evidence for the facts than against.

PROBATE   *Probate* is a court procedure in which a court determines the existence of a valid Will and then supervises the distribution of the Probate Estate of the decedent.

PROBATE ESTATE   The *Probate Estate* is that part of the decedent's Estate that is subject to probate. It includes property that the decedent owned in his name only. It does not include property that was jointly held by the decedent and someone else. It does not include property held "in trust for" or "for the benefit of" someone.

PRO BONO The term *Pro Bono* means "for the public good." When an attorney works Pro Bono, he does so voluntarily and without pay.

REAL PROPERTY   *Real property,* also known as *real estate,* is land and anything permanently attached to the land such as buildings and fences.

REMAINDER INTEREST A *Remainder Interest* in real property is the property that passes to the holder of the Remainder Interest once the owner of the Life Estate dies.

RESIDUARY BENEFICIARY A *residuary beneficiary* of a Will is a beneficiary who is entitled to whatever is left of the Probate Estate once the specific gifts made in the Will have been distributed and once the decedent's bills, taxes and costs of Probate have been paid. If there is more than one residuary beneficiary, then they share equally in the residuary Estate, unless the Will provides for a different distribution.

RESOURCE   A *resource* for purposes of determining Medicaid eligibility, is an asset owned by the decedent, or his spouse, that can be converted to meet their needs. Federal statute 42 U.S.C. 1382b identifies what is (and is not) counted as a resource.

REVOCABLE LIVING TRUST   A *Revocable Living Trust* (also known as a *Inter Vivos Trust*) is a Trust that is created and becomes effective during the lifetime of the Settlor (or Grantor). A *revocable* Trust is one which can be amended or revoked by the Grantor or Settlor during his lifetime.

SETTLOR A *Settlor* or a *Trustor* is someone who creates a Trust.

SOLE PROPRIETORSHIP   A *Sole Proprietorship* is a form of business ownership in which one person owns all of the assets of the business and that person is personally liable for all of the debts of the business

SPENDTHRIFT A *Spendthrift* is someone who wastes money and/or spends lavishly.

SPENDTHRIFT TRUST A *Spendthrift Trust* is a Trust created to provide monies for the living expenses of a beneficiary, and at the same time protect the monies from being taken by the creditors of the beneficiary.

STEPPED-UP BASIS A *stepped-up basis* is the value placed on property that is acquired in a transaction such as inheriting property or purchasing property. The "step-up" refers to the increase in value of basis from the basis of former owner (usually what he paid for it), to the basis of the new owner (usually the market value when the transfer is made).

SURROGATE A *surrogate* is a substitute; someone who acts in place of another. In New York, the *Surrogate's Court* handles Probate matters.

TENANCY BY THE ENTIRETY A *Tenancy by the Entirety* is the name of a form of ownership of real property held by a husband and wife. It is a joint tenancy with right of survivorship, modified by the common law theory that the husband and wife are one. With a joint tenancy with right of survivor, each joint tenant owns their own share of the property until death, when the surviving owner owns it 100%. With a Tenancy by the Entirety, each owns 100% of the property both before and after death.

TENANCY IN COMMON *Tenancy In Common* is a form of ownership such that each tenant owns his/her share without any claim to that share by the other tenants. Unlike a joint tenancy, there is no right of survivorship.

TITLE INSURANCE *Title Insurance* is a policy issued by a title company after searching title to the property. The insurance covers losses that result from a defect of title, such as unpaid taxes, or someone with a claim of ownership of the property.

TRUST AGREEMENT A *Trust agreement* is a document in which someone (the Grantor or Settlor) creates a Trust and appoints a Trustee to manage property placed into the Trust. The usual purpose of the Trust is to benefit persons or charities named by the Grantor as beneficiaries of the Trust.

TRUSTEE A *Trustee* is a person, or institution, who accepts the duty of caring for property for the benefit of another.

UNASSIGNABLE ANNUITY An *unassignable annuity* is an annuity that cannot be assigned; i.e., the annuitant's benefits cannot be transferred to another.

WAIVER A *waiver* is the intentional and voluntary giving up of a known right.

WARRANTY DEED A *Warranty Deed* is a deed in which the Grantor warrants (promises) that the property he is transferring has good and clear title; i.e., that no one else has rights in the property. This is different than a *Quit-claim Deed* where the Grantor says, in effect, "I am releasing any interest I have in this property to you, but I make no guarantees about anyone else's right to this property."

INDEX

A

B

C

A Will is Not Enough in New York

W

116 NEW YORK STATUTES & CODES are referenced in
A Will Is Not Enough In New York

Each state has its own set of laws relating to the control, and protection of a person's Estate. The New York laws relating to Guardianship, Probate and especially Medicaid are very different from the laws of other states.

The author is in the process of "translating" *A Will Is Not Enough* for the rest of the states; that is, to write a book that incorporates the laws of the state into a book that describes how to prepare an Estate Plan appropriate to the residents of a given state.

A Will Is Not Enough is now available for the following states:
    California, New York, New Jersey, Maryland and Virginia

To check whether this book is currently available for other states call Eagle Publishing Company of Boca at
(800) 824-0823
or visit our Web site http://www.eaglepublishing.com

SPECIAL OFFER FOR PURCHASERS OF THIS BOOK
$25 INCLUDES SHIPPING

To order call (800) 824-0823

Guiding Those Left Behind

Amelia E. Pohl has written a series of books explaining how to settle an Estate. Each book is state specific, telling how things are done in that state. Each book explains:

- ✧ who to notify
- ✧ how to locate the decedent's property
- ✧ how to get possession of the inheritance
- ✧ when you do, and do not, need an attorney
- ✧ the rights of a beneficiary, and much more.

Each book is written with the assistance of an experienced attorney who is licensed and is practicing in that state.

The ***Guiding*** series is currently available for the following states: ALABAMA, ARIZONA, CALIFORNIA, FLORIDA
GEORGIA, ILLINOIS, INDIANA,
MASSACHUSETTS, MARYLAND, MICHIGAN
MINNESOTA, MISSOURI, NEW JERSEY,
NEW YORK, NORTH CAROLINA, OHIO, PENNSYLVANIA
SOUTH CAROLINA, TENNESSEE, TEXAS, VIRGINIA
WASHINGTON, WISCONSIN

Connecticut, Mississippi, Kentucky and Hawaii are scheduled for release in 2003.

Visit our Web site http://www.eaglepublishing.com
to check whether books for other states are available at this time.

SPECIAL OFFER FOR PURCHASERS OF THIS BOOK
$20 INCLUDES SHIPPING

To order call (800) 824-0823

BOOK REVIEWS FOR GUIDING THOSE LEFT BEHIND

ARIZONA

Ben T. Traywick of the Tombstone Epitaph said "This book is an excellent reference book that simplifies all the necessary tasks that must be done when there is a death in the family. There is even an explanation as to how you can arrange your own estate so that your heirs will not be left with a multitude of nagging problems." "This reviewer has been going through probate for two years with no end yet in sight. This book at the beginning, two years ago, would have helped immensely."

CALIFORNIA

Margot Petit Nichols of the Carmel Pine Cone called it a "...TRULY RIVETING READ." "... I could scarcely put it down." "This is a book that we should all have, either on our book shelves or thoughtfully placed with our important papers."

FLORIDA

Maryhelen Clague of the Tampa Tribune Times wrote "Amelia Pohl has created a handy, self-help guide that illustrates the necessary steps that must be taken when someone dies, a guide that is easy to read, extremely clear and simple to refer to when the need arises."

TEXAS

Lois Scott of the Victoria Advocate wrote "I think this is a most valuable book that each family should have on hand. One never knows when it might be needed suddenly."

It is the goal of EAGLE PUBLISHING COMPANY to keep our publications fresh.

As we receive information about changes to the federal or New York law we will post an update to this edition at our Web site:

http://www.eaglepublishing.com